The Origins Of The Messianic Ideal

Robert Wolfe

J-REP

Published by J-REP
jeyrep@compuserve.com

 Produced at The Print Center, Inc., 225 Varick St.,
New York, NY 10014, a non-profit facility for literary and arts-related publications. (212) 206-8465

Table Of Contents

"Compared to what we might have known had the records of the human past not mostly vanished, we can learn little from ten existing documents of one vanished king, from fifty of another, or yet a thousand of another. We do not, in effect, possess the wholeness of history, but only some of its pages - and a historian faces his severest challenges when he attempts to grasp the silences that lie between them. For this goal, philology and analysis of texts are only preliminary tools aiding another process. This consists not in whimsy or fantasy, nor in the imagination of the painter or poet, but rather in the synthesis of new ideas regarding the historical unknown, made from separately experienced elements: the faculty, that is, by which we attempt to reconstruct what is absent. Except for those narrow historical works that only recite the barest known facts, there are none that do not require this mental synthesis - and no process is more difficult for the historian to master or use judiciously."

Norman Golb, *Who Wrote The Dead Sea Scrolls?*, page xv

"Yet let no empty gust
Of passion find an utterance in thy lay,
A blast that whirls the dust
Along the howling street and dies away;
But feelings of calm power and mighty sweep.
Like currents journeying through the windless deep."

William Cullen Bryant
1794-1878

"To penetrate deep into complexities, it is essential to focus one's sights on a single subject."

Amnon Cohen, *Jewish Life Under Islam*, page viii

Introduction

The purpose of this book is to reconstruct the origins of the Messianic ideal. By the term, "Messianic ideal", I mean the concept of "the Messiah" that took shape in Jewish culture during the period from roughly 200 BCE to 200 CE. Although this concept has exerted a tremendous influence on world history and culture, little is known of its origins apart from what can be inferred from a number of texts. These can be grouped into five main categories:

- The prophetic books of the Jewish Scriptures, most particularly the Book of Isaiah. This can be seen as the first major statement of what was to become the Messianic ideal.

- The so-called "intertestamental writings", or "Apocrypha and Pseudepigrapha", of the period 200 BCE to 200 CE. Most of the Dead Sea scrolls also belong in this category. These texts are probably the most important source for an understanding of the origins of the Messianic ideal.

- The New Testament, particularly the four gospels.

- The writings of Josephus. These writings are virtually the only narrative source for the history of the Jewish people in the land of Israel during the period 200 BCE to 100 CE.

- Scattered references to "the Messiah" in the Mishnah, Gemara and Talmud. These references indicate the existence of a fully formed concept of "the Messiah" which had come into being in Jewish culture starting in the 3rd century CE.

Entirely absent from this list is any text which actually discusses how and why the Messianic ideal came into being. Josephus was not interested in this question and the other texts simply depict this ideal in one form or another without linking it to any particular political or religious tendency. Moreover, little or nothing is known about the authors of these texts, including the authors of the four gospels. Hence we know a good deal about who "the Messiah" was supposed to be but almost nothing about the people who developed and popularized this concept. Most of the texts which express the Messianic ideal cannot even be dated with any precision or assigned to any particular place of origin.

Over and above the objective difficulty of reconstructing the origins of the Messianic ideal from these essentially anonymous texts, there is also a subjective difficulty. There exists a certain disinclination on the part of both Christian and Jewish historians to investigate the origins of the Messianic ideal because of the role which this ideal has played in the history of both religions. Christianity is founded on the assertion that Jesus Christ was "the Messiah". This assertion is embedded in the very words, "Jesus Christ", which represent the Greek form of a term which would appear as "Yeshua Mashiach" in Hebrew or "Joshua Messiah" in English. But precisely because it is so essential for Christianity that Joshua be named Messiah, Christians are none too eager to view "the Messiah" as a concept which originated in the same way as any other concept, through a gradual historical process. Their preference is to view "the Messiah" as an ideal which fell from the skies, which was revealed to the Jewish people as an intimation of the Savior who was to come. They don't always express this preference in so many words, but they reveal their disinclination to view the Messianic ideal as a product of Jewish history by not writing numerous historical studies of its origins.

Jewish historians are more open to a historical approach to the Messianic ideal, but here too an obstacle presents itself. For the past 2000 years, the expectation of the coming of "the Messiah" has played an important role in Jewish history. As a rule, the stronger this expectation, the greater the disinclination to view the Messianic ideal as a product of history. Just like the Christians, only for slightly different reasons, Orthodox Jews want to think of this ideal as something that fell from the skies, as a prefiguring of the Redeemer who is to come. Secular Jewish historians may not share this belief, but because of the strong feelings of the Orthodox on this point, there exists a certain reluctance even among secular Jewish historians to investigate the origins of the Messianic ideal in the same way as they would investigate the origins of any other ideal.

Ultimately the subjective difficulty of understanding the origins of the Messianic ideal is built into the ideal itself. From the start, this ideal assumed the form of a prediction of the advent of a great leader. For all those who believed in the accuracy of the prediction, it was essential that it appear not as the product of the mere hopes and aspirations of those who enunciated it but rather as a valid prophecy of a predetermined future event, a prophecy which was vouchsafed to its prophets by supernatural means. To treat the Messianic ideal as the outgrowth of a historical process is therefore in some sense to challenge the ideal itself, and that is not something that is done lightly. For all of these reasons, there are surprisingly few historical studies which attempt to understand the Messianic ideal in terms of the social, political and ideological background of those who created it.

Most of what has been written on this subject has appeared within the past fifty years. *The Messianic Idea In Israel* by Joseph Klausner and *He That Cometh* by Sigmund Mowinckel were the first historical studies in English to deal with the origins of the Messianic ideal in any detail. Both books were published in the early 1950s, although Klausner's book included material which he had published earlier. Klausner was a distinguished Israeli historian, Mowinckel a Norwegian Protestant theologian. Klausner noted, on page 5, that a comprehensive study of the origins of the Messianic ideal "has not yet been written". He did take note of a short book by Julius Greenstone entitled *The Messiah Idea In Jewish History* which had appeared in 1906 but felt it was "too brief and summarizing" to be of much value.

Klausner and Mowinckel both adopted the same method, which was to survey the Jewish literature of the 1st millenium BCE in an effort to depict the slow development and evolution of the Messianic ideal. Neither author showed any interest whatsoever in the social movements of the period, nor did they utilize any other sources save for literary ones. Nonetheless both authors made a valuable contribution to the understanding of the Messianic ideal as the product of history, albeit an exclusively literary history. To be sure, Mowinckel's book was somewhat marred by a constant effort to project Christian doctrines backward into the early history of the Jewish Messianic ideal. Thus, for example, he argued on page 62 that the Jews in the days of the monarchy believed in the "divinity" of their king, which was based on their conviction that he was the "son" of "Yahweh". All the same, the fact that Mowinckel viewed the Messianic ideal as growing out of a long historical process was still a major step forward for a devout Christian such as he was.

Yet despite the pathbreaking efforts of Klausner and Mowinckel, the literature on the origins of the Messianic ideal remained rather sparse for the next thirty years or so. The great Jewish historian Gershom Scholem published a collection of essays entitled *The Messianic Idea in Judaism* in 1971, but most of his attention was devoted to the role of the Messianic idea in Kabbalah, a subject on which he was and is the leading authority. However Scholem could not resist saying a few words on the origins of the Messianic ideal, which he did in the first essay in the collection, "Toward an Understanding of the Messianic Idea in Judaism". Scholem stated on page 5:

> The predictions and messages of the biblical prophets came to an equal degree from revelation and from the suffering and desperation of those whom they addressed; they are spoken from situations and again and again have proven effective in situations where the End, perceived in the immediate future, was thought about to break in abruptly at any moment.

Scholem's point was that the notion of "the End", or what he called "apocalypticism", was the key to the Messianic ideal. Scholem also distinguished between what he called "utopian" and "restorative" Messianism, and this distinction was widely cited by later writers. But like Klausner and Mowinckel, Scholem did not even address the question of why "apocalyptic" and "utopian" elements should have been so much more prominent in Jewish tradition than in the traditions of other peoples.

It is only in the past twenty years that issues of this kind have begun to be raised by historians of the Messianic ideal. Although no major books have been written on this topic, an extensive monographic literature has come into being which explores specific issues in great detail. Characteristic of the historical studies that have appeared in recent decades is *The Messiah*, edited by the Christian scholar James Charlesworth and published in 1992. It is a collection of papers delivered at the "First Princeton Symposium on Judaism and Christian Origins". In his paper, "The Concepts of *Masiah* and Messianism In Early Judaism", S. Talmon states on page 81:

> Initially the *masiah* idea is an intrinsically sociopolitical no-
> tion which must be assessed primarily in the historical set-
> ting and the conceptual context of the biblical institution of
> kingship. Also in its later manifestations, it can be best
> evaluated in the framework of constituted groups that
> present to the viewer a specific socioreligious profile.

Unfortunately, Talmon did not actually do this in his article, nor has any other writer attempted a comprehensive study of the origins of the Messianic ideal in terms of the "specific socioreligious profile" of the "constituted groups" that espoused it.

Indeed, some recent writers have even begun to question whether there ever was any such thing as a Messianic ideal. This is the position adopted by Jacob Neusner in *Messiah In Context*, published in 1984. Neusner sees this ideal as a "composite" which was more or less invented by historians such as Klausner and Scholem. He states specifically on page 227:

> Klausner and Scholem provide portraits of a composite text
> that, in fact, never existed in any one book, time, or place, or
> in the imagination of any one social group, except an imag-
> ined "Israel" or a made-up "Judaism".

This stance is in keeping with the recent tendency to focus on specific issues relating to the history of the Messianic ideal while avoiding any kind of comprehensive or systematic treatment of the subject. Neusner also wanted to prove that Judaism is not a "messianic religion" even though it "contains numerous allusions to a Messiah and references to what he will do". Yet on Neusner's own showing, the concept of "the Messiah" was an integral part of rabbinic Judaism and enjoyed canonical status throughout the period from the composition of the Talmud down to modern times.

Surveying the existing literature on the origins of the Messianic ideal, certain points may be said to have been definitely established. In the first place, it is clear that the belief in the Messiah grew out of the sufferings of the Jewish people. This point was already clear to Julius Greenstone, who wrote in 1906 on page 23 of *The Messiah Idea In Jewish History*: "It was perfectly natural that a people with such a past should long for a happier future, when there would be an end to their sufferings."

In the second place, it is clear that this belief developed gradually, beginning with the prophets, continuing with the radical Jewish movements of the Second Temple period and culminating in the establishment of a canonical doctrine of "the Messiah" in both Christianity and Judaism. This gradual process stretched over a period of approximately 1000 years, beginning in the early 1st millenium BCE and ending in the early 1st millenium CE.

In the third place, it is clear that the Messianic ideal was associated with a whole set of other ideas, which can be grouped together, as Scholem did, under the heading of "apocalypticism". Among the notions which can be included under this heading is a belief in the resurrection of the dead at the time of the "end of days" or "last judgment". At this time it is believed that sinners will be condemned to everlasting punishment while the righteous will receive their heavenly reward. In Jewish tradition the Messianic ideal was also invariably associated with the expectation of the establishment or restoration of an ideal Jewish state in the land of Israel.

What is mainly lacking in the existing literature is a clear understanding of how and why the Messianic ideal developed as it did. Most writers on this topic act as if the Messianic ideal evolved from one book to another, without reference to the social movements and groups which espoused and popularized it. The unspoken reason why they adopt this approach is because most of them accept the traditional view that the Messianic ideal was vouchsafed to the Jewish prophets through divine revelation. As Mowinckel put it on page 138 with reference to the origins of the Messianic ideal: "Ultimately it is rooted in the experience of God which came to an Isaiah, a Jeremiah, or a Deutero-Isaiah." Even Scholem in the passage cited above saw "revelation" as equally important to "suffering and desperation" as an explanation for the origins of Jewish Messianism. This may constitute an explanation in the eyes of true believers, but from the standpoint of secular historiography it is no explanation at all.

Joseph Klausner, whose book, *The Messianic Idea In Israel*, is still probably the most important single work on this topic, openly admitted that he was opposed to a "materialist" understanding of Jewish Messianism. On page x of his Preface, he bemoaned the lack of "prophetic idealism" in the Israel of his day in the following terms:

> But alas! it is not the Hebraic, the prophetic, the Messianic-Israelitic social conception which has become a basis for bringing about redemption in the land of vision and promise, but a foreign social conception, linked up with economic and historical materialism, to which the prophetic idealism is a mockery.

Other writers were not so candid, but a systematic bias in favor of religious belief is characteristic of the great bulk of the literature on Jewish Messianism. This literature is generally secular in tone but not in spirit. And conversely, thoroughly secular writers tend to shy away from the subject of the Jewish Messianic ideal, which they seem to view as an irrelevant distraction from the serious business of studying popular social movements.

Consider for example the treatment of the Messianic ideal by Doron Mendels in *The Rise And Fall Of Jewish Nationalism*, published in 1992. Mendels, a professor of ancient history at the Hebrew University of Jerusalem, sought to develop a comprehensive picture of the Jewish nationalism of the Second Temple era in this book. No one doubts that the Messianic ideal was a key component of the Jewish nationalism of this era, yet Mendels devotes only six pages to the subject in a book of over 400 pages. What he does have to say in these six pages is superficial and misleading. He distinguishes between "political" and "transcendental" conceptions of "the Messiah", adding with reference to the latter: "For this concept we are almost solely dependent on the New Testament". This is simply not true: the "apocryphal" and "pseudepigraphal" works which Mendels cites throughout his book are filled with references to a "transcendental" Messiah. It is evident that Mendels just didn't want to deal with the subject of the Messianic ideal and therefore dismissed it as briefly and completely as he could.

What fascinates the religious and challenges the secular about the Messianic ideal is its inspirational quality. It is entirely reasonable and even necessary to treat the Messianic ideal as just one facet of the Jewish national movement of ancient times, and yet experience has shown that it is a very important facet indeed. No less an authority than David Ben-Gurion, the founder of the modern state of Israel, testified to its importance in an interview with Moshe Pearlman. Asked by Pearlman how the Jewish people was able to preserve its identity during 2000 years of exile, Ben-Gurion replied as follows, on page 225 of *Ben Gurion Looks Back*:

> I am convinced that its preservation was due to the constant and all-pervasive awareness of Jews throughout the centuries of something I can only express in a seemingly archaic phrase - the *vision of Messianic redemption*, national and all-human. By this I mean their own redemption, their restoration as a sovereign people in their old land and their moral elevation to model nationhood, and the redemption of all humanity, the triumph of peace, righteousness and equality in the world and the conquest of tyranny and wickedness. This twin idea of the Messianic vision informs the whole of Jewish history and the Jewish faith. It is the core of the religious, moral and national consciousness of the Jewish people.

And if we add to the picture the influence which Messianic movements in a Christian or Muslim context have exerted on world history, the power of the Messianic ideal becomes apparent. But crediting this power to a non-existent invisible entity called God in no way explains it. The explanation must rather be sought in the history of the Jewish people during the period when the Messianic ideal germinated, developed and became established as an integral part of both Judaism and Christianity.

What is really at issue here is the place of the Jewish people in world history. It is no coincidence that so little was written on the origins of the Messianic ideal prior to the founding of the state of Israel. Viewing this ideal as exclusively the product of a divine revelation fit in with an arrogant, contemptuous attitude towards the Jewish people, such as was prevalent in scholarly circles as well as elsewhere prior to the birth of Israel. And even after Israel was founded, it was primarily Jewish historians, many of them Israelis, who led the way in developing a more realistic view of the origins of the Messianic ideal. Only in recent decades have a significant number of Christian scholars also begun to see the Messianic ideal in a more realistic light. And even now this realism has its limits, for the complete abandonment of a supernatural explanation for the origins of the Messianic ideal would require a recognition of the important role which the Jewish people has played and continues to play in world history.

In Christian and also to some extent in Jewish historiography, the notion of divine revelation has made it possible to view the Jewish people as the unworthy vehicle of a non-Jewish supernatural force. Eliminating the notion of divine revelation has the effect of placing the Jewish people at the center of the historical process which gave rise to the Messianic ideal. If this ideal has merit, then the Jewish people must have merit too. But the source of this merit must be sought in the real history of the Jewish people and not in myth or legend. In short, a completely realistic, objective treatment of the origins of the Messianic ideal is the only possible basis for understanding the long history of heroism and self sacrifice from which this ideal was derived. It was because literally millions of people fought and died in the name of this ideal that it became such a powerful force in world history. It is to these nameless millions that this book is dedicated.

Chapter One: Prophecy

If the history of the Messianic ideal may be said to begin anywhere, it begins with prophecy. In Jewish literature, the Messiah was almost invariably described in the form of a prophecy of a great leader who was to appear at some future time. The first such predictions appear in the prophetic books of the Jewish Scriptures, and in particular in the Book of Isaiah. So who was Isaiah, and who were the Hebrew prophets, and why did they place such emphasis on making predictions?

The key to understanding the Hebrew prophets is to understand the Hebrews. The account of Hebrew origins contained in the Torah contains too many mythological elements to provide an appropriate starting point for understanding the Hebrews. The most appropriate starting point is the large number of written records emanating from the Middle East and dating from the 2nd millenium BCE which make some reference to people known variously as Habiru, Apiru or Epiru. This material was surveyed by Moshe Greenberg in his article, "The Hab/piru", appearing in 1955 in the *American Oriental Series*, Volume 39. Greenberg noted that Habiru in different places were variously described as bandits, mercenaries, day laborers or runaway slaves. He concluded that they were "economically destitute" fugitives who had grouped themselves into organized bands which camped on the outskirts of the more settled areas in the Middle East. Texts referring to Habiru have been unearthed in Iraq, Syria, Turkey, Lebanon, Israel and Egypt, making it clear that they constituted a social class rather than a tribe or nation. Or as Greenberg put it on page 65: "Originating in widely scattered localities, bearing names of several linguistic backgrounds, little more than a common status can be said to unite them."

For the past 50 years and more, a debate has raged among "Biblical scholars" as to whether or not the Hebrews of the Torah were Habiru. The only reason why there is any doubt on this point is because the Torah depicts the early Hebrews as a tribe or nation, not a social class. However the evidence linking the Hebrews and Habiru is overwhelming. In the Egyptian archives unearthed at Tel al-Amarna there are numerous references to large numbers of Habiru present in Canaan in the 14th century BCE. These references may be found in the two volume collection, *The Tell El-Amarna Tablets*, edited by Samuel Mercer. The Habiru are described as a serious military force who were taking part in a rebellion againt Egyptian rule in Canaan. There are also Egyptian records which make reference to Habiru seized as prisoners by the Egyptians, Habiru transported to Egypt by their Egyptian captors and Habiru working as slaves on building projects for the Egyptians. In the light of this evidence, it is apparent that the story of Hebrew origins contained in the Torah must be discounted as a typical patrilineal myth of origins -12 tribes from the 12 sons of one father. The Hebrews who fled from Egypt were clearly Habiru, who subsequently joined forces with other Habiru bands in Canaan and conquered it.

Habiru rule in Canaan was based on the teachings of Moses, an Egyptian notable of some kind who had joined the Habiru after fleeing into the Sinai. These teachings represented a synthesis between the Egyptian conception of God - a wise He in the sky who had created the universe and ruled over it - with the egalitarian, rebellious spirit of the Habiru. What made this synthesis possible was a heavy stress on the Law, symbolized by the stone tablets on which the Ten Commandments were engraved and sanctified by the authority of God. The Law defined the Habiru as a band of brothers, whose unity was to be upheld through the irreversible rite of circumcision. The Law mandated obedience to God but also the redistribution of property every 50 years and a ban on the return of runaway slaves (Deuteronomy, Chapter 23). The Law of Moses proved an appropriate ideology for Hebrew rule in Canaan, and in time the Hebrews came to think of themselves as a band of brothers in a literal as well as a figurative sense.

In this way they metamorphosed into the ruling class of the land of Israel. This process took perhaps 200 years, from the time of Moses to the time of David and Solomon. The ruling class of David's kingdom differed from the typical ruling class of most countries at that time in two significant ways. It had emerged from a class of fugitive slaves, and it was able to preserve the laws and traditions of that class in the form of detailed texts utilizing alphabetical writing. There is every indication that alphabetical writing was first developed by Canaanite stone workers, probably slaves of the Egyptians, working in the Sinai desert during the 2nd millenium BCE. The first known alphabetical writings appear on stones in the Sinai, and it was undoubtedly also Canaanite stone workers who inscribed the stone tablets of the Hebrew Law which legend later portrayed as received by Moses from God in that very same Sinai. The writing system which the stone workers devised was derived from Egyptian hieroglyphics but constructed entirely out of sounds which were represented by over twenty symbols called letters. Alphabetical writing was a proletarian invention, and taken together with the proletarian origins of the Hebrew ruling class, it gave Hebrew ruling class culture a unique character relative to other ruling class cultures.

This culture was more literate and more radical than most ruling class cultures of that day. At the same time it was also highly nationalistic. Hebrew was the spoken language of the common people of Canaan, while the previous ruling class of Canaan had been dominated by Hittites from the north and Egyptians from the south. The previous rulers of Canaan had written in Accadian hieroglyphics, an established Middle Eastern writing system derived from Iraq, whose use was discontinued by the Hebrews. Hebrew culture evolved in large part out of Canaanite popular culture, but it defined the Hebrews as an elite, set apart by circumcision, assigned by God to rule over Canaan. Hebrew ruling class culture was thus resolutely ruling class, and in this it resembled the ruling class culture of most countries. The clearest expression of this resemblance was the concept of God, which was found in some form in most kingdoms of that day.

The writings of Isaiah and the other Hebrew prophets grew out this tradition. What made these writings unusual and memorable was that same unique blend of ruling class and populist attitudes which characterized Hebrew culture in general. The prophets were monarchists, supporters of the kings of the house of David, yet at the same time, they were also populists, upholders of the egalitarian tradition created by the Habiru. Max Polley brings out this connection in great detail in *Amos And The Davidic Empire*. Amos was the author of the famous lines, "But let justice well up as waters, and righteousness as a mighty stream." Polley notes, on page 112, that Amos was "the

16

first classical prophet to champion the cause of the poor and the needy in the land". Yet he was also a staunch supporter of the rule of the kings of Judah and denounced the kingdom of Israel and also the surrounding kingdoms of Edom, Moab, Ammon, Damascus, Philistia and Tyre for refusing to accept Davidic rule. In the mind of the prophets, argues Polley on page 122, Davidic rule and justice for the poor were linked by "the ideal of the just king". This ideal, which they associated with David and Solomon, "became the basis for the messianic hope of the postexilic period". Of all the prophets who enunciated this ideal, none proved more influential than Isaiah.

Isaiah

Isaiah created his ideal in the form of a prediction. Chapter 11 of the Book of Isaiah begins with the well known lines:

> And there shall come forth a shoot out of the stock of Jesse,
> And a twig shall grow forth out of his roots.
> And the spirit of the Lord shall rest upon him,
> The spirit of wisdom and understanding,
> The spirit of counsel and might,
> The spirit of knowledge and of the fear of the Lord.
> And his delight shall be in the fear of the Lord;
> And he shall not judge after the sight of his eyes,
> Neither decide after the hearing of his ears;
> But with righteousness shall he judge the poor,
> And decide with equity for the meek of the land;
> And he shall smite the land with the rod of his mouth,
> And with the breath of his lips shall he slay the wicked.
> And righteousness shall be the girdle of his loins,
> And faithfulness the girdle of his reins.
> And the wolf shall dwell with the lamb,
> And the leopard shall lie down with the kid;
> And the calf and the young lion and the fatling together;
> And a little child shall lead them.

Jesse was the father of David, so the reference to "a shoot out of the stock of Jesse" made it clear that the awaited leader would be a descendant of David. Christian tradition has treated these lines as a prophecy of the advent of Jesus Christ, but it makes more sense to treat the image of Jesus Christ in the New Testament as an effort to conform to the prophecy of Isaiah. In any case there can be no doubt that these lines represent the beginning of a tradition which eventually came to be known as Messianic.

Just what did Isaiah really have in mind? Yehoshua Gitay deals with this question at length in *Isaiah and his Audience*, published in 1991. Isaiah lived during the latter part of the 8th century BCE, at a time when the survival of both Judah and Israel was threatened by the rising power of Assyria. Most of the first 39 chapters of the Book of Isaiah, which the majority of scholars believe are the only chapters which were actually written by Isaiah, were written during the reign of king Ahaz of Judah. Isaiah wanted Ahaz to pursue a policy of neutrality relative to Assyria, neither accepting Assyrian rule nor aligning with those kingdoms, such as Israel, that wanted to form an anti-Assyrian coalition. Isaiah felt that Ahaz was too pro-Assyrian, and Gitay argues that Isaiah's image of the ideal king of Judah was intended as a subtle rebuke to Ahaz. Gitay speaks of Isaiah's writings as follows, on page 234:

> He emphasizes the high qualities of the new Davidic king who will be a charismatic king, inspired directly by God. The king will thus avoid human error (a reference to the present king, Ahaz, who did not listen to Isaiah's previous advice concerning the war).

Gitay sees Isaiah as first and foremost a political thinker, whose writings "are basically concerned with one central topic, the meaning of world political affairs."

However, as Gitay recognizes, Isaiah was also a moralist. He saw Assyrian influence as responsible for the moral corruption of Judah's rulers and therefore associated his policy of neutrality relative to Assyria with a program of moral and spiritual regeneration. The task of the future ideal king was to implement this program. Moreover, Isaiah was not only a moralist but an idealist. He dreamt of a better world, one which has never been and perhaps will never be. Yet literally billions of people over time have been influenced by his vision, which has remained fixed in the mind of many long after the conflcts between Judah, Israel and Assyria have been forgotten. What

18

Isaiah was really saying is that the path to survival for Judah lay in the triumph of the ideal of peace and justice everywhere. Unfortunately, this triumph has been a long time in coming, and in the meanwhile the kingdom of Judah was overthrown by the Babylonians about 150 years after the time of Isaiah. But perhaps in some ultimate sense Isaiah was right, for the Jewish people survived the fall of the kingdom of Judah in 586 BCE and has continued the struggle for peace and justice on a world scale with some success right down to the present day. As a prophet Isaiah was not very successful, but as a political agitator he was without peer.

He was such a good agitator that he inspired later prophets to speak in his name. Most scholars believe that chapters 40 to 55 of the Book of Isaiah were written not long after the fall of Judah by someone whom the scholars have dubbed "Deutero-Isaiah", meaning the second Isaiah. This second Isaiah introduced a new figure into the Book of Isaiah, one whom the scholars have dubbed "the Suffering Servant". He is described as follows, in chapter 53 of the Book of Isaiah, in the translation of the Jewish Publication Society of America:

> He was despised, and forsaken of men,
> A man of pains, and acquainted with disease,
> And as one from whom men hide their face:
> He was despised, and we esteemed him not.
> Surely our diseases he did bear, and our pains he carried;
> Whereas we did esteem him stricken,
> Smitten of God, and afflicted.
> But he was wounded because of our transgressions,
> He was crushed because of our iniquities:
> The chastisement of our welfare was upon him,
> And with his stripes we were healed.

It would seem that the authors of the New Testament drew heavily upon the image of "the Suffering Servant", as well as the image of the ideal king created by the first Isaiah, in creating their portrait of Jesus Christ. But "the Suffering Servant" is not presented as an ideal king by the second Isaiah, rather as a prophetic figure whose suffering is ultimately the result of exile and defeat. Mowinckel, on page 219 of *He That Cometh*, sees him as inaugurating "a new ideal of prophecy: not the diviner, but the missionary preacher of true religion."

19

Scholarly opinion is divided as to whether the concluding chapters of the Book of Isaiah, chapters 56 to 66, were written by the second Isaiah or by yet a third prophet also speaking in the name of Isaiah. The concluding chapters revert to the predictive mode of the early chapters, proclaiming the advent of an end to exile and the restoration of Jerusalem to its former glory:

> For, behold, I create new heavens
> And a new earth;
> And the former things shall not be remembered,
> Nor come into mind.
> But be ye glad and rejoice for ever
> In that which I create;
> For, behold, I create Jerusalem a rejoicing,
> And her people a joy.

Thus speaks "the Lord" in chapter 65, but no more is heard here of an ideal king. Instead a new voice is introduced, one which is heard in chapter 63:

> I have trodden the winepress alone,
> And of the peoples there was no man with Me:
> Yes, I trod them in Mine anger,
> And trampled them in My fury;
> And their lifeblood is dashed against My garments,
> And I have stained all My raiment.
> For the day of vengeance that was in My heart,
> And My year of redemption are come.
> And I looked, and there was none to help
> And I beheld in astonishment, and there was none to
>   uphold;
> Therefore Mine own arm brought salvation unto Me,
> And My fury, it upheld Me.

This translation makes it appear that the voice is that of "the Lord", but there are no capital letters in the Hebrew original, nor is the voice specifically identified as that of "the Lord". The imagery is certainly more human than divine, and it is entirely possible to read this passage as the voice of a warrior conjured up by "Isaiah" to avenge the sufferings of the Jewish people and bring an end to exile and defeat.

Be that as it may, it is evident that the various authors of the

Book of Isaiah (and some scholars posit more than two or three) had differing conceptions of the ideal leader for the nation of Judah. There are nonetheless certain themes which run throughout the entire book and make it possible to read it as the work of a single author, which is what most people did prior to the rise of modern "Biblical scholarship". In particular, the ideal leader is consistently portrayed as a unique and solitary individual. He is called on to deal with the threat of annihilation facing the nation of Judah and he does so in a spectacular manner. As a result of his actions, not only is the nation saved but a new era is ushered in, one of unprecedented peace and harmony. These are the characteristic themes of the Jewish Messianic tradition and run throughout its entire history. If anyone may be said to be the founder of this tradition, it is most certainly Isaiah, or more precisely, "Isaiah".

However, the ideal leader is not called "the Messiah" in the Book of Isaiah, nor is there any attempt to present belief in his coming as an article of faith. Furthermore, since the actual prophecies of "Isaiah" did not materialize, the Book of Isaiah did not enjoy anything resembling canonical status in Jewish culture for many centuries after its composition. It was a popular work, numerous copies of which were found among the Dead Sea scrolls, but that is all. As numerous authors have already pointed out, the image of the Jewish people as collectively awaiting the appearance of "the Messiah" at the end of the 1st millenium BCE is essentially a Christian myth. The Book of Isaiah was composed during a period of roughly 200 years stretching from the start of the Assyrian invasions in the 8th century BCE to the rebuilding of the Temple in the 6th century BCE. It represented an appropriate although somewhat utopian attempt to deal with the threat to Jewish survival posed by the Assyrians and Babylonians, but thanks to the Persians, the Jewish people did survive this threat. It is true that the appearance of a new and even more deadly threat posed by the Greeks and Romans led to a revival of Messianic agitation at the end of the 1st millenium BCE, but even then, belief in the coming of "the Messiah" did not immediately become an article of faith. Isaiah did not create a canonical faith in "the Messiah", but what he did do was to create a way of articulating this faith. This way was called prophecy.

The Prophets

Not many details are known about the social background of the Hebrew prophets. Isaiah came from a "noble family", as is noted in the entry under his name in Geoffrey Wigoder's *Encyclopedic Dictionary of Judaica*. The relationship with the kings of Judah maintained by the Hebrew prophets suggests that most of them came from a somewhat similar background. The prophets generally related on terms of social equality with the kings of Judah. They often acted as unofficial advisers to the kings, and their writings grew out of this social function.

David Ben-Gurion stressed this aspect of prophecy in his essay, "The Monarchy and the Prophethood", which appears in *Ben-Gurion Looks At The Bible*. Speaking of the prophets from Amos to Jeremiah, whom he called the "Literary Prophets", Ben-Gurion stated on page 304:

> These prophets not only preached against the moral and social decadence, and about the people's tendency toward foreign gods, but they were also seasoned philosophers on political and national matters. They were not only familiar with what went on among the people, but also with what was happening among neighboring nations. There were some among them whose understanding of political and international affairs was superior to that of the king, his officers, and his advisers.

Ben-Gurion added, on page 305, that the prophets also "demanded belief in one God, God of heaven and earth, and preached truth and justice, mercy and righteousness, assistance for the needy, the orphan, and the widow." These are the themes which most commentators have emphasized in discussing the prophets, but it is evident that their moral and religious pronouncements formed a part of a larger world outlook which was intended to deal with the pressing political and diplomatic issues confronting the ruling class of Judah.

Ben-Gurion also noted that the first person to be called a "prophet" in Hebrew tradition was none other than Moses himself. The last sentence in the Book of Deuteronomy, which is the last book of the Torah, begins with the words, "And there arose not a prophet since in Israel like unto Moses, whom the Lord knew face to face". The Hebrew word for "prophet" which is used here is "navie", the same term which is generally used to describe the "Literary Prophets", including Isaiah. The fact that Moses was called a "prophet" is significant because Moses in the Torah is never described as making predictions. At least in English, the word "prophet" basically means "someone who makes predictions". The Hebrew term "navie" also has this connotation, but obviously it is not essential to its meaning. The root meaning of "navie" is someone who speaks the truth, who says what must be done, who articulates the path of righteousness and survival for the people. Among the Hebrews, a woman could also be a "prophet" (or "naviah"), and Deborah and Huldah are so described in the Hebrew Scriptures. Whether a man or a woman, a prophet was basically defined as a speaker, or as Ben-Gurion put it: "In the Torah, a spokesman - someone who is capable of speaking about, and explaining things - is called a prophet."

The key figure in shaping the role of the prophet in Hebrew culture was undoubtedly the prophet Samuel. Samuel lived at the time of the founding of the Hebrew monarchy by Saul and David. He was a judge as well as a prophet and occupied a position of some importance in Hebrew society prior to the founding of the monarchy. He was far from enthusiastic about the concept of monarchy and offered the following prediction, in chapter 8 of the first Book of Samuel, to the "people that asked of him a king":

> This will be the manner of the king that shall reign over you: he will take your sons, and appoint them unto him, for his chariots, and to be his horsemen; and they shall run before his chariots. And he will appoint them unto him for captains of thousands, and captains of fifties; and to plow his ground, and to reap his harvest, and to make his instruments of war, and the instruments of his chariots. And he will take your daughters to be perfumers, and to be cooks, and to be bakers. And he will take your fields, and your vineyards, and your oliveyards, even the best of them, and give them to his servants...And ye shall cry out in that day because of your king whom ye shall have chosen you; and the Lord will not answer you in that day.

But despite his misgivings Samuel accepted first Saul and then David as kings because he saw no other way to cope with the Philistine menace. He inaugurated the tradition in which the prophet functioned both as the supporter and the critic of the kings of Judah. The important point is that his authority did not stem from that of the kings but, to the contrary, predated and preceded it. The tradition which he founded assumed a kind of division of labor between king and prophet, with the king responsible for war and government, the prophet for giving advice and moralizing.

Giving advice and moralizing did not necessarily require making predictions, but as time went on, making predictions became an increasingly important part of the prophet's role. Samuel couched his advice to the "people that asked of him a king" in the form of a prediction, but he was really offering a warning rather than seeking to describe some predetermined future event. Moreover, it is far from certain whether Samuel really spoke the words cited above or whether they were invented by later chroniclers in order to demonstrate how farsighted he was. It was the prophet's responsibility to be farsighted, and for this reason accurate predictions came to be expected of the prophets. However most of the resulting predictions were not unlike the prognosis which a contemporary historian or social scientist might offer regarding future trends. They relied more on factual information and common sense than on pure intuition and divine inspiration. But from the start the prophets also claimed divine inspiration, and there is a whole school of thought among scholars which seeks to associate the Hebrew prophets with modern studies of "shamanism". This approach is legitimate, but only if it is recognized that "shamans" too often functioned as moralists and political advisers in their original tribal setting.

The really big question that has to be confronted here is: just what basis in fact, if any, is there for the belief that the Hebrew prophets were the recipients of divine inspiration? It is evident that the universe, by definition, is all there is. It is infinite in time and space and therefore could neither be created by nor ruled by any invisible entity separate and apart from itself. However, just because a revelation is not divine doesn't mean that it can't be a revelation. It would seem that Sitting Bull really did have a vision of "many soldiers falling into camp" the night before Custer's assault at the Little Big Horn. My own experience and the experience of others convinces me that there is such a thing as intuitive knowledge of the future that may appear in dreams or visions. It is reasonable to assume that the Hebrew prophets had a pronounced capacity for intuitive knowledge of the future. This capacity, buttressed by the wealth of factual information and political experience which they possessed, enabled them to make predictions that seemed realistic and plausible to their contemporaries. Few of these predictions actually did come true in any literal sense, but they often accurately described future trends and tendencies. And the accuracy of these descriptions was also enhanced by the increasingly popular practice of writing in predictions after the fact to describe events which had already happened.

In this way arose the cult of predictions that is so evident in the Book of Isaiah. This cult may be said to be the foundation of the Messianic faith. The Messiah began as the Someone who would appear at some future date as specified in a prophetic prediction. The various authors of the Book of Isaiah could not quite agree on just who this Someone was supposed to be, but they all put great stock in the expectation of his coming. So in its origins, faith in the Messiah was a way of expressing faith in the prophets. Those who were animated by such a faith gradually formed a prophetic party. The prophets were opposed to a warlike foreign policy, critical of the sacrifice of animals required by the Temple ceremonies and solicitous of the rights of the people. These teachings were more popular in the cities than in the countryside, and in the cities they were most popular among small merchants and artisans. The party to which they gave rise eventually came to be known as the Pharisee party, which was in turn the forerunner of rabbinical Judaism.

From the start the Christians invested so much time and effort in discrediting the Pharisees that it has become difficult for anyone to notice that it was these very same Pharisees who were the main supporters and upholders of the prophetic tradition on which Christianity itself was founded. The legalism of the Pharisees, of which the Christians were so critical, was a direct outgrowth of the prophetic tradition. It was the prophets who first taught that if only the Jewish people would observe the commandments of the Jewish religion, then they would be rescued from foreign domination by a miraculous Savior. The Pharisees perpetuated this belief, which was far from commanding the support of the entire Jewish people. The whole point of the famous legalism of the Pharisees was precisely to make sure that a Savior would arise. The Pharisees venerated the writings of the prophets, made copies which they circulated among the people and placed these writings in a special category second only in importance to the Torah itself. What is called the "Old Testament" by Christians is known in Hebrew as "Tanach", which is an acronym for "Torah", "Neviim" (Prophets) and "Cotvim" (Writings, meaning everything else). This usage derives from the special status which the Pharisees assigned to the writings of the prophets, a status which was perpetuated and enhanced in rabbinicial Judaism.

Louis Finkelstein describes the transition from the prophets to the Pharisees as follows on page 3 of *The Pharisees*:

> The social forces which had made the patrician landowner of the eleventh century B.C.E. desert the YHWH of his nomadic ancestors and worship the *baalim* of the earlier Canaanite agriculturalists, and had driven his successors of the sixth century B.C.E., to imitate Assyrian and Egyptian manners, dress and worship, produced the Hellenist in the third century B.C.E., as well as the Sadducee and the Herodian of a later generation. Conversely, the follower of the prophet gave way to the Hasid, and the latter was succeeded by the Pharisee.

Finkelstein also noted, on page 344, that the typical Jewish farmer was an "uncompromising nationalist", while the urban plebeian was a "liberal universalist" and the patrician "a perpetual opportunist". Liberal universalism was a religious ideology created by the prophets and spread by the Pharisees in the urban areas, first of Judah, and later of the entire Mediterranean region. What came to be known as the cult of the Messiah grew out of this ideology and was, from the start, an essential part of it. But in the beginning it was not called the cult of "the Messiah", nor was there anything resembling an established view of exactly who the awaited Savior was supposed to be. The Book of Isaiah was too complex and eclectic to provide any such view. What was needed was a real life leader, and he appeared with Judah the Maccabee.

Judah

Judah the Maccabee was not a "shoot out of the stock of Jesse", nor did he work any miracles, but he did what Isaiah's awaited Savior was supposed to do, drive out the foreigners and restore the Jewish religion. Not since the time of David had there been a Jewish leader who had a comparable impact on the political life of the Jewish people. As if to confirm his Messianic vocation, rabbinical tradition eventually invented a miracle to credit him with, the so-called "miracle of the lights", according to which the oil which he used to relight the menorah in the Temple burned for eight nights when there was seemingly only enough oil for one. There is no mention of this miracle in the first or second Book of the Maccabees, which were written soon after the events which they describe, and it was not until many hundreds of years after his death that the first reference to the "miracle of the lights" appeared in rabbinical literature. But from the start, the figure of Judah the Maccabee exercised a powerful influence on the imagination of the Jewish people, setting in motion a political upheaval which was to culminate in the emergence of the cult of "the Messiah".

From the 6th to the 2nd century BCE, the former kingdom of Judah had formed a part of the successive Babylonian, Persian and Greek empires. Prophecy in the traditional sense of the term ceased because there was no longer any Jewish king for the prophet to advise. But under the Persians, the Jewish people had been permitted to rebuild the Temple which the Babylonians had destroyed. The High Priests of the second Temple, who claimed descent from Zadok, the first High Priest, acted in many ways as the rulers of the Jewish people. They did not command an army, such as the kings of Judah had done, but they did exercise great authority in cultural and religious matters. The Persians actually encouraged this authority, and initially the Greeks at least tolerated it. But under the rule of Antioches Epiphanes in the 2nd century BCE, the Greeks attempted to take over the Temple in Jerusalem and institute their own ceremonies there. They also sought to ban all Jewish religious ceremonies, with the avowed intention of "Hellenizing" the Jews and transforming Jerusalem into a Greek "polis". Jews who resisted were killed, and the remaining Jews were threatened with annihilation if they did not accept Greek supremacy.

It was at this time that the Maccabees arose, under the leadership of Judah the Maccabee, and drove the arrogant Greeks out of the Temple. They led a guerilla army which liberated Jerusalem, and although Judah the Maccabee was killed in battle only a few years after his great victory, his brothers continued the struggle and eventually drove out the Greeks from the greater part of the former kingdoms both of Judah and of Israel. The anniversary of the relighting of the menorah in the Temple by the forces of Judah the Macabee was proclaimed a national holiday by the Maccabees, giving rise to the Jewish holiday of Hanukah, which is celebrated for eight days starting on the 25th of Kislev. Not even David has a Jewish holiday in his honor. The Maccabees chose to make this holiday eight days long because Succot, the big fall festival, is also eight days long. And since Succot was one of the three annual festivals on which Jews were expected to gather in Jerusalem, making Hanukah equivalent to Succot was a way of underlining the importance that the Maccabees attached to its celebration. It was originally celebrated by lighting oil lamps for eight days in succession; later, in Europe, the oil was replaced by candles.

The association of oil and Hanukah is also emphasized in Jewish tradition by the custom of eating potato pancakes or doughnuts cooked in oil during the eight days of the holiday. A relevant fact in this context is that the Hebrew word "Mashiach", from which the English word "Messiah" is derived, stems from a Hebrew root which means "to anoint with oil". Another relevant fact is that the later Maccabees were actually anointed with oil as part of the ceremony confirming them as rulers of the Jewish people. Their status as rulers was formally endorsed by a "Great Assembly" of the Jewish people in 141 BCE. According to Solomon Zeitlin, on page 148 of Volume 1 of *The Rise and Fall of the Judaean State,* the Maccabean ruler, Simon, at that time received the civil title of "Sar Am-El", "Prince of the People of God". At the same time he was also confirmed as High Priest of the Temple in Jerusalem, a position first claimed by Judah the

Maccabee's brother, Jonathan. Finally, at the end of the 1st century BCE, the Maccabees also began to formally claim the title of "king" of Judah, while continuing to hold the title of High Priest. If ever there was a theocracy, this was one. And it was from this theocracy that there emerged the cult of "the Messiah".

The precise time and place at which this cult may be said to have originated is at that same "Great Assembly" in 141 BCE when it insisted on an addendum to the decree making Simon "Prince of the People of God" and "High Priest" at one and the same time. The addendum, notes Zeitlin, still on page 148, specified that Simon could continue in both offices only until a "true prophet" should arise. The implication was that at that time Simon or one of his descendants would relinquish the office of High Priest. This was an open invitation to Messianic agitation. And since the Maccabees sought to combine political and religious authority in one person, there was a certain tendency for images of the anticipated "true prophet" to assume a similar form. He would of course become High Priest, but the High Priests had also exercised the function of rulers of the Jewish people under the Persian and early Greek empires. Just as the Maccabees were essentially military leaders who also claimed religious authority, so the anticipated "true prophet" could be pictured as a religious leader who also claimed political authority. And lurking behind both versions, the Maccabean and the prophetic, was the actual figure of Judah the Maccabee, the victorious warrior and defender of the faith, who had given his life at a young age to save his country.

One historian who has stressed this point is William Reuben Farmer, author of *Maccabees, Zealots, and Josephus*. Farmer concluded on page 203 that "the example and teaching of the Maccabees probably exerted a much greater influence on Jews during the New Testament period than is generally recognized." Farmer noted that most of the leaders "of seditious activity against Rome" bore the same names as those of the early Maccabees, including Judah of Galilee, the rebel leader whom Josephus viewed as the founder of the Zealot movement. Farmer emphasized the continuity between the image of the early Maccabees as religious leaders and later Messianic movements. He put it this way, on page 48:

> Jewish nationalism in the Roman period, in our view, was
> not secular. Nor was it, properly speaking, ethnocentric.
> Rather, as in the Maccabean period, it was theocentric.

However, Judah the Maccabee was the only member of the Maccabee family (also known as the Hasmoneans) who was universally admired by later Jewish writers. After his time the Maccabean and prophetic traditions diverged, and this divergence was formally recognized by the decree of the "Great Assembly" in 141 BCE anticipating the replacement of the Maccabean High Priests by a "true prophet".

Typical of the type of speculation which this decree encouraged is the following passage from the "Testaments Of The Twelve Patriarchs", a "pseudepigraphal" work thought to date from the early 1st century BCE. It may be found in Volume 1 of *The Old Testament Pseudepigrapha*, edited by James Charlesworth. On page 794 appears the following prediction:

> And then the Lord will raise up a new priest
> to whom all the words of the Lord will be revealed.
> He shall effect the judgment of truth over the earth for many
>   days.
> And his star shall rise in heaven like a king;
> kindling the light of knowledge as day is illumined by the
>   sun.
> And he shall be extolled by the whole inhabited world.
> This one will shine forth like the sun in the earth;
> he shall take away all darkness from under heaven,
> and there shall be peace in all the earth.

And so forth and so on. It is easy to see why this work was preserved in a Greek language form by Christian copyists, who also inserted minor "interpolations" of their own. The more disillusioned the followers of the prophetic tradition became with the later Maccabees, the more glowing became their description of the anticipated "true prophet" who was to replace them as High Priest.

The Pharisees were the leaders of the prophetic opposition to the Maccabees during the 2nd and 1st centuries BCE. The term "Pharisee" does not appear in rabbinical literature; it is a term which was applied to the Pharisees by others and has a dual meaning in

Hebrew. The Hebrew word, "Perushim", from which the English term "Pharisees" is derived, comes from a root which conveys the meaning both of "interpretation" and "separation". The Pharisees were known as "interpreters" of the Law, but they were also viewed by their Maccabean critics as "separatists", divisive factionalists whose agitation for the removal of the Maccabees as High Priests was undermining the unity of the Jewish people. And in fact the Pharisees did go so far as to collaborate with first the Seleucid Greeks and then the Romans in their efforts to overthrow Maccabean rule in the land of Israel. The politics of the Pharisees, which flowed from their pacifist outlook, led them to harshly condemn the Jewish militarism of the Maccabees while simultaneously striving to appease the much more militaristic Greeks and Romans. They feared an unsuccessful Jewish revolt, which could and did result in the total devastation of the land of Israel. Yet at the same time, the Pharisees refused to accept the cultural domination of the Greeks and Romans, which they viewed as an unacceptable alternative to the Jewish religion. They dreamed of an autonomous kingdom of Judah, but since they had no faith in the military future of the Maccabees and Zealots, they had to put their faith in a miraculous future. In this way they were led into the world of Messianic phantasies and apocalyptic expectations.

Apocalypse

Apocalyptic expectations were the logical outcome of the predictive mode. And the popularity of this mode was itself the result of two key factors. One was the experience of decline and defeat, beginning with the Assyrian and Babylonian invasions; the other was the prior experience of victory and success, as epitomized by the formation of the Davidic kingdom. The fact that the Hebrews had once triumphed over their foes created the expectation that this success could be repeated; and the fact that this expectation was not being realized in the present made it necessary to imagine its realization at some future time. These were the factors that inspired the prophetic tradition in the first place, and then with the victory of Judah Maccabee, the prophetic tradition appeared vindicated. For a period of approximately 300 years after the time of Judah Maccabee, from the middle of the 2nd century BCE to the middle of the 2nd century CE, a constant stream of literary works in the predictive mode therefore issued forth from Jewish writers in the land of Israel.

One of the first of these works, and the only one to be included in Tanach (the so-called Old Testament) by later rabbinical authorities, was the Book of Daniel. It is generally thought to date from the middle of the 2nd century BCE, perhaps from the time of Judah Maccabee himself. It concludes with the following prophecy, at the beginning of chapter 12:

> And at that time shall Michael stand up, the great prince who standeth for the children of thy people; and there shall be a time of trouble, such as never was since there was a nation even to that same time; and at that time thy people shall be delivered, every one that shall be found written in the book. And many of them that sleep in the dust of the earth shall awake, some to everlasting life, and some to reproaches and everlasting abhorrence. And they that are wise shall shine as the brightness of the firmament; and they that turn the many to righteousness as the stars for ever and ever.

In later years, the notion that the dead would be resurrected at the end of time became a standard part of the rabbinical conception of "The World To Come". This notion is also found in a number of later "apocryphal" and "pseudepigraphal" works, including some of the Dead Sea scrolls. However, there is still no reference to "the Messiah" in the Book of Daniel. His role is played by Michael, "the great prince who standeth for the children of thy people", who was later viewed in rabbinic tradition as an "angel" of God.

Prophecies such as this were both the cause and the consequence of the real life Jewish struggle for national independence and cultural autonomy. There would have been no prophecies had not actual leaders emerged from time to time who realized these goals in whole or in part. On the other hand, literary prophecies undoubtedly played a role in encouraging these leaders to arise and strive to live up to the great expectations embedded in the prophetic books. However, it would seem that the prophecy writers and the prophecy fulfillers were not always the same type of people. This divergence contributed to the tension between the Pharisees, who were the chief guardians of the literary culture, and the Maccabees and Zealots, who led the fight for political independence against the Greeks and Romans. But precisely because the Pharisees wrote, edited or preserved most of the literary works on which subsequent historians have relied for their picture of early Jewish history, it is their viewpoint and not that of the Maccabees and Zealots which tends to dominate historical study of the so-called "Intertestamental Period".

The only path to a true understanding of the origins of the Messianic ideal is to see it as the outgrowth of a complex dialectic between two equally valid and legitimate tendencies, a prophetic and apocalyptic tradition on the one hand, and a political and military tradition on the other. Every serious historian who has written on this subject has recognized the dual character of the Messianic ideal. Perhaps Joseph Klausner put it best when he stated, on page 392 of *The Messianic Idea In Israel*:

> In the course of the long evolution of the Jewish Messianic idea, two different conceptions were inseparably woven together: politico-national salvation and religio-spiritual redemption. These two elements walked arm in arm. The Messiah must be both *king* and *redeemer*. He must overthrow the enemies of Israel, establish the kingdom of Israel, and rebuild the Temple; and at the same time he must reform the world through the Kingdom of God, root out idolatry from the world, proclaim the one and only God to all, put an end to sin, and be wise, pious and just as no man had been before him or ever would be after him.

But what most historians have refused to recognize is that both the prophetic and the military components of the Messianic ideal had their origin in the revolutionary militarism of the runaway slaves known as Habiru. It was ultimately because both strands of the Messianic tradition had the same origin that they remained "arm in arm" throughout their entire history.

Moreover, most historians have followed the Pharisees in tending to favor the prophetic over the military element in the Messianic tradition. The later Maccabees are typically viewed as unscrupulous Hellenizers, just as the Pharisees thought them to be. No hint appears in most historical studies of just what the Maccabee perception of the Pharisees might have been. The only negative image of the Pharisees that ever appears is the one created by the Christians, who were even more extreme than the Pharisees in their preference for the prophetic over the military component in Jewish Messianism. And everyone seems to forget that the spectacle of a victorious king of Judah presiding over the religious rites of the famed Jewish temple in Jerusalem must have exerted quite an influence on the political imagination of the surrounding region. The fact that the Jewish temple did not contain the image of a god or goddess was known throughout not only the Middle East but the entire Mediterranean region. It stood for something that has come to be called "monotheism", which has now swept the world in a Christian or Muslim guise. But before there was Christianity or Islam there was the religion of the Maccabees, and it is this religion which we must understand if we wish to truly understand the origins of the Messianic ideal.

Chapter Two: Sects

In place of the religion of the Maccabees, what appears in the historical literature are "sects". The religion of the Pharisees is defined as the normative Judaism of the second Temple period, and all other versions of Jewish thought and belief are lumped together under the heading of "sects". Worse yet, the Maccabees are not even assigned a sect of their own but are forced to lurk somewhere in the background of the recognized sects such as the Sadducees and Zealots. The unspoken assumption behind this procedure is that the religion of the Maccabees was not really a religion at all but just an excuse to control the Temple. And many Pharisees undoubtedly thought just this, but it is unlikely that most Jews at that time would have agreed with them. Most Jews in the land of Israel at that time lived not in the cities but in the countryside, and it was there that the religion of the Maccabees had its roots.

All historiography has a built in bias in favor of the cities over the countryside. The authors of written records generally lived in the cities rather than the countryside, and the physical remains uncovered by archaeologists, such as buildings or sculptures, also usually emanate from the cities. We know that until very recently the great majority of the human race lived in the countryside rather than in the cities, but since this great majority has left us few written records or physical remains, it tends to get overlooked in the history books. This is all the more true with reference to early Jewish history, because the Pharisees, who compiled most of the written sources, had a definite prejudice against people from the countryside. Louis Finkelstein, on page 76 of *The Pharisees*, speculates that the Pharisees got their name, which can mean "Separatists" in Hebrew, from their emphasis on "separation from impurity and defilement". According to Finkelstein, who was a great admirer of the Pharisees, the Pharisees were mainly concerned with separating themselves from the "am ha-aretz", the "people of the land", whom they viewed as the epitome of "impurity and defilement". Members of the Pharisee "Order" or "Society" were not permitted to eat with "people of the land"; doing so was considered grounds for expulsion from the group. In later rabbinical tradition, the term, "people of the land", became a standard expression for people who were ignorant and boorish, as many country people undoubtedly were, at least in the eyes of the Pharisees and rabbis.

The rebellion of the Maccabees started in a town called Modiin, which is located in the foothills of the rocky slopes which lead up from the coastal plain to Jerusalem. The terrain is flat enough to be conducive to agriculture yet hilly and wooded enough to conceal the guerilla forces which the Maccabees led. These forces were mainly recruited from the nearby countryside. At the core of the religion of the Maccabees was the simple historical fact that the military victory of the Maccabees over the Greeks was also a triumph of rural over urban classes. But since it was the urban classes who wrote most of the literature subsequently venerated in rabbinical tradition, the triumph of the Maccabees was not remembered in these terms. It was remembered rather as a victory of the Jewish religion over Greek paganism. The later Maccabees were then depicted as having deviated from the Jewish religion in the direction of paganism, necessitating the corrective action of the true believers, the Pharisees. However, in the eyes of the Maccabees, it was the Pharisees who constituted a sect, whereas the Maccabean religion was the legitimate one, consecrated by history and tradition.

The great achievement of the Maccabean army of farmers was the conquest of Jerusalem and the establishment of Jewish military control over the Temple Mount. This control was not relinquished for 100 years. The Maccabean rulers were first and foremost responsible for control of the Temple Mount. Their religious function as High Priests derived from this military function. This synthesis of military and religious authority was something new in Jewish culture. In Judah prior to the Babylonian captivity, military and religious authority had been divided between the Davidic line of kings and the Zadokite priestly dynasty. And following the Babylonian captivity, under first Persian and then Greek rule, no independent Jewish military authority had existed. The highest Jewish authority was the High Priest, confirming the status of the Temple in Jerusalem as the main symbol of Jewish independence. It was in large part for this reason that the Maccabees first sought to become High Priests, and only later claimed the title of king as well. They essentially created a new office, that of the high priest as military leader. Only Moses had previously occupied a comparable position in Jewish history, and Moses had left no heirs.

What is today remembered of this office is mainly that the Pharisees objected to it. The ideology which must have once existed in order to justify this office in the eyes of the Maccabees and their supporters has disappeared from sight, to be replaced in official historical memory by the "sects". A common feature of most of these "sects" is their emphasis on issues relating to the ceremonies conducted on the Temple Mount. And since the Maccabees were in control of the Temple Mount during the period when most of these "sects" first flourished, it would seem likely that there must have been some connection between the Maccabees and the "sects". But according to official historical memory, the only connection was a negative one. The "sects" are thought to have been hostile to the Maccabees. For example, some of the Dead Sea scrolls speak of a "Wicked Priest" who persecuted the "Teacher of Righteousness", and for years the leading experts on the Dead Sea scrolls maintained that the "Wicked Priest" must have been a Maccabean king, perhaps Alexander Janneus or one of his predecessors.

Only recently has this view been challenged. In 1999 three scholars, Michael Wise, Martin Abegg Jr. and Edward Cook, published a revised and updated translation of the Dead Sea scrolls entitled, *The Dead Sea Scrolls: A New Translation*. In their introduction, they developed the view that the "sect" which compiled the Dead Sea scrolls was actually in favor of the policies of the Maccabean kings and hostile to the Pharisees. They pointed out, on page 23, that the latest archaeological findings indicate that Qumran, where the Dead Sea scrolls were found, was "founded by the Hasmoneans, not by the Essenes" and was situated "right in the middle of a line of fortresses established by the Hasmonean dynasty", meaning the Maccabees. They note that one of the scrolls, which appears on page 399, is written in praise of "Jonathan, the king", whom they identify with Alexander Janneus. They identify the "Wicked Priest" with Hyrcanus 2, who was of Maccabean descent but allied himself with the Pharisees after the death of Alexander Janneus and permitted them to persecute the followers of his brother, the Maccabean king Aristobulus

2. These findings suggest that much of the literature of the "sects", which was previously viewed as either indifferent or hostile to Maccabean rule, may in fact have reflected a Maccabean point of view, one which has yet to be reconstructed in detail.

Reconstructing the religion of the Maccabees requires rediscovering it in the literature of the "sects". This is the literature of the Dead Sea scrolls, of the "apocryphal" and "pseudepigraphal" texts, and of course, of early Christianity, which originated as a "sect" of Judaism. And like the other "sects", Christianity can easily be seen as pro-Maccabean. It was the Christians, after all, who preserved the First and Second Book of the Maccabees after these books had been excluded from the Jewish Scriptures by the rabbis. Despite their systematic hostility to most manifestations of Jewish nationalism, the Christians have always had a soft spot for Judah the Maccabee. The most likely explanation for this soft spot is the central role which the religion of the Maccabees seems to have played in the emergence of the Messianic ideal. The literature of the "sects" is permeated with this ideal, which could even be described as the most characteristic feature of "sectarian" ideology. All the "sects" claimed to await a Redeemer, though of the most varied kind. This was a role embodied by the Maccabees, in relation to whom all other conceptions of a Redeemer were inevitably measured.

The Dead Sea Scrolls

Of all the "sects", the one that has attracted the greatest scholarly attention in recent decades is the one associated with the Dead Sea scrolls. For 40 years and more, a debate has raged in scholarly circles over the precise nature of the group or groups which deposited many hundreds of scrolls for safekeeping in caves overlooking the Dead Sea. Most authorities originally assumed that this group was identical to a quasi-monastic sect called "Essenes" which was known from descriptions in the works of Josephus and Pliny. Pliny said that the Essenes lived by the shores of the Dead Sea, which is where the scrolls were found. But in recent years, an increasing amount of evidence has been brought forward indicating that Qumran, the ancient building site close to where the scrolls were found, was a

Maccabean fortress and not a monastic retreat. The clearest proof of who wrote the scrolls ought to be what they say, but this too is in dispute, as most are in fragmentary condition missing many portions. People mentioned in the scrolls are rarely referred to by name but rather by code words such as "the Wicked Priest", "the Teacher of Righteousness", "the Flattery Seekers", "the Lion of Wrath" and "the Men of the Lie". A small cottage industry has come into being manufacturing theories as to who wrote these words and what they mean.

Relative to earlier Jewish writings, the Dead Sea scrolls are more "religious". Much of the material in Tanach consists of historical or legendary accounts of actual events. The Dead Sea scrolls contain hardly any works of this kind, but rather exhortations, prayers, rules, denunciations and commentaries - in short, "religious" literature. The expectation of a future Redeemer pervades this literature, motivates it and validates it. But there is no great focus on the person of the anticipated Redeemer, who is sometimes called "Mashiach", sometimes other names, sometimes merely implied, but generally assumed. The focus is rather on the entire set of circumstances which will surround his appearance - the revival of the dead, the day of judgment, eternal life for the faithful, eternal damnation for the evildoers. Those who nurture these expectations are "sons of light"; those who do not are "sons of darkness". There is a war between them, and in the end the "sons of light" will win under the able leadership of the Lord of Hosts. In the meanwhile, it is necessary to follow the rules, which were evidently numerous. It does not seem unreasonable to describe this belief system as the creation of a sect, particularly in view of the many scrolls which refer to the use of a new solar calendar intended to replace or supplement the traditional Jewish lunar calendar.

References to the new solar calendar are so numerous that the editors of *The Dead Sea Scrolls: A New Translation* state, on page 25:

> The doctrine that God had commanded Israel to follow a 364-day solar calendar instead of a 354-day lunar calendar was a key tenet of the Qumran group. This peculiar calendar unifies the scrolls more than any other single sectarian element.

The existence of this calendar was already known prior to the discovery of the Dead Sea scrolls due to references to it in several "pseudepigraphal" works, particularly the Book of Jubilees. But until the discovery and translation of the Dead Sea scrolls, it was unclear whether anyone had actually attempted to use the calendar described in the Book of Jubilees. The scrolls make it clear that this calendar was in daily use at Qumran. As the editors note on page 297, "adherence to a peculiar calendar is the thread that runs through hundreds of Dead Sea scrolls". Some scrolls try to synchronize the new solar calendar with the old lunar calendar, but most appear to follow the line of the Book of Jubilees, which condemned the lunar calendar as inaccurate.

As it so happens, in actual fact it was the new solar calendar which was inaccurate. It was based on a solar year of only 364 days, which meant that it would fall behind the actual cycle of the seasons by one and a quarter days every year. After approximately 25 years it would be a month behind, and after 100 years four months behind. What these figures indicate is that the new solar calendar could not have been used for a very long time and still retained its credibility. This means that the scrolls which endorse it must all have been composed within a relatively short span of time not much longer than 25 years or so. And since most of the few specific events which are mentioned or alluded to in the Dead Sea scrolls date from the period 76 to 63 BCE, it would seem likely that most of the scrolls were composed during this period or shortly thereafter. As the editors point out on page 313, this was "a time of tremendous upheaval in Jewish society". It was a period which witnessed a sharp division within the Maccabean ranks, one faction making peace with the Pharisees, the other continuing to oppose them. The authors of the Dead Sea scrolls clearly sided with the anti-Pharisee faction and accused the Pharisees of persecuting them. These considerations suggest that the most obvious and likely explanation of the Dead Sea scrolls is that they were written by supporters of the Maccabees who were forced into semi-exile by the Dead Sea as a result of the split in the Maccabean ranks.

This theory is supported by a passage in *Jewish Antiquities* by Josephus. The split in the Maccabean ranks took place after the death of Alexander Janneus in 76 BCE. His widow, Salome Alexandra, and son Hyrcanus then formed an alliance with the Pharisees, while his other son, Aristobulus, sought to perpetuate the anti-Pharisee policies of his father. The Pharisees demanded that the supporters of Alexander Janneus who had taken part in the execution of Pharisee leaders during his lifetime should now themselves be executed. Some were put to death, but Aristobulus then intervened and insisted that the remainder be spared. A description of what happened next appears on page 451 of *The New Complete Works of Josephus*. The threatened supporters of Alexander Janneus told Salome Alexandra that "if she had determined to prefer the Pharisees, they still insisted that she would place them everyone in her fortresses; for if some fatal demon has a constant spite against Alexander's house, they would be willing to bear their part, and to live in a private station there." According to Josephus, Salome Alexandra agreed to this request. And since Qumran has been shown to be a Maccabean fortress, one which was situated in a barren desert some distance from any settled area, it seems entirely plausible that some or all of the remaining supporters of Alexander Janneus should have been sent there as a kind of semi-exile.

The Maccabees were soldiers and Alexander Janneus was the most successful soldier of them all. He extended the boundaries of his kingdom of Judah to roughly the same extent as the boundaries of David's kingdom of Judah. His hard core followers, the ones who had taken part in the execution of hundreds of Pharisees on his orders, may safely be assumed to have also been soldiers. At the same time, the evidence of the Dead Sea scrolls makes it clear that many of them, and especially their leaders, were priests. It is very likely that they constituted some kind of combined priestly and military force associated with the physical control of the Temple Mount. Exiled to Qumran, it was only natural for them to reconstitute themselves as a sect. Their military mindset permeates the Dead Sea scrolls, and in particular the well known "War Scroll", which sets forth the scenario for the impending final battle of the "sons of light" with the "sons of darkness" in great detail. The following passage from the "War Scroll" appears on page 161 of *The Dead Sea Scrolls: A New Translation*:

> Rise up, O Hero, take Your captives, O Glorious One, take Your plunder, O You who do valiantly lay Your hand upon the neck of Your enemies, and Your foot upon the backs of the slain. Crush the nations, Your adversaries, and may Your sword devour guilty flesh. Fill Your land with glory, and Your inheritance with blessing.

Just so had Alexander Janneus actually done, and just so did his exiled priestly soldiers undoubtedly hope to do when their opportunity might arise.

In the meanwhile they sought to perfect their organization, which is about all they could do living in semi-exile at Qumran. A "Teacher of Righteousness" arose, rules were laid down, penalties were exacted. It may have been at this point that they adopted the new solar calendar. Why did they do this? Calendars are about holidays, and Jewish holidays at that time were celebrated first and foremost at the Temple Mount. When Salome Alexandra and the Pharisees formed their alliance, the Pharisees gained control of the calendar and assumed responsibility for setting the dates of Jewish holidays. The former guardians of the Temple Mount evidently used the new solar calendar as a way of disputing this control. They declared that the Pharisee dates were inexact and only the solar dates were exact. In so doing they sought to set themselves up as the ideological rivals of the Pharisees. And like all rivals, they did not hesitate to incorporate elements of their opponent's thinking into their own ideology. Their vision of the "last days" did not greatly differ from the Pharisee vision. And in fact, neither vision greatly differed from a vision which was commonplace in Middle Eastern culture under the name of Zoroastrianism.

Zoroastrianism was the official religion of the Persian empire, and it taught that there would come a Day of Judgment and a Final Battle in which Good would triumph over Evil. The dead would be resurrected and all would receive their appropriate reward. This was not a traditional Jewish belief. Only in a few of the later books of Tanach is there even so much as a hint of Hebrew interest in any alleged life after death. This belief entered Judaism under Persian influence during the period when Judah was a part of the Persian empire. And throughout its history, this belief has been associated with a solar calendar. The Egyptians, who originated this belief, used a solar calendar, and both the Persians and the Romans, who eventually adopted similar beliefs, also adopted solar calendars. Life after death and solar calendars went together because both were associated with belief in a supreme central authority. Adoption of a solar calendar by the exiles at Qumran had a similar implication of an assertion of authority over Jewish life in general and the Temple Mount in particular. The exiles saw the Pharisees asserting their own version of religious authority in alliance with Hyrcanus and Salome Alexandra, and they sought to compose a counter-version that could successfully compete with that of the Pharisees. But as fate would have it, their counter-version ended up buried in jars, while the Pharisee version went on to become rabbinical Judaism.

The cause of the exiles at Qumran was doomed by the arrival of the Roman legions around 63 BCE. Aristobulus and his followers waged a determined resistance against the Roman invaders, but they were defeated and dispersed. However, during the period between 76 and 63 BCE and perhaps for some time thereafter, the sect that had formed at Qumran seems to have represented a significant force in Jewish politics. It was not confined to Qumran but had branches elsewhere. One of the best known of the Dead Sea scrolls is commonly called "The Damascus Document". It was already known from a copy found in the Jewish quarter of Cairo and published in 1910. It is a manifesto of "those entering the new covenant in the land of Damascus". Damascus was at that time under the rule of the Nabatean Arabs, who had overthrown Greek rule there around 85 BCE. Alexander Janneus had enjoyed good relations with the Nabatean king, Aretas, and the exiles at Qumran evidently established a branch in his territory. Evidence of their ties with Aretas is provided by Josephus, who says that before the followers of Alexander Janneus asked to be placed in a fortress, they had told Salome Alexandra that "Aretas, the Arabian king, and the monarchs, would give any reward, if they could get such men [meaning themselves] as foreign reinforcements, to whom their very names, before their voices be heard, may perhaps be terrible". They asked to be sent to Aretas, and only when this request was rejected did they agree to accept exile in a fortress.

"The Damascus Document" follows the same line as the other

scrolls, warning that "it is not permitted to celebrate the holidays too early or too late", suggesting adherence to the new solar calendar. It also states, on page 58 of *The Dead Sea Scrolls: A New Translation*, that sinners will be struck down by the sword "when the Messiah of Aaron and of Israel comes". This phrase, "the Messiah of Aaron and of Israel", is repeated a number of times in "The Damascus Document", indicating that it was in common use. Among those who will be struck down by "the Messiah of Aaron and of Israel" are the "Boundary-Shifters" and the "Shoddy-Wall-Builders". It seems very likely that the Dead Sea scrolls were the first Jewish writings in which the term, "the Messiah", was used in what was to become its standard sense of an awaited Redeemer who will do Great Things. For the exiles at Qumran, these Great Things were essentially the Maccabean Great Things: defeat the enemy, control the Temple, perform religious rituals. The stress on religious rituals was reflected in the reference to Aaron, who was considered the founder of the Jewish priesthood. The exiles were obviously dissatisfied with Hyracanus as a High Priest, and awaited his replacement with "the Messiah of Aaron and of Israel". But instead of the Messiah it was the Romans who arrived, and many of the members of the Qumran sect undoubtedly perished in the 20 years of fighting that ensued before Judah was temporarily "pacified" with the aid of Herod.

The Messiah whom they anticipated is notable for his transparency. In not one scroll is there even a hint of any attempt to describe the Messiah or say anything about him except that he was anticipated. The contrast with the lengthy descriptions in the Book of Isaiah could not be more complete. Notable also is the absence of any attempt to associate the Messiah with descent from David. This was also Maccabean, for the Maccabees were not descended from David yet they claimed the title of king of Judah. But it does not seem probable that the sect at Qumran equated "the Messiah of Aaron and of Israel" with the current Maccabean king, Aristobulus, who had failed to prevent the execution of a number of their comrades by Salome Alexandra and Hyrcanus. They probably awaited a new Judah the Maccabee, a new "Hero" who would lead them to victory. And because this hope was disappointed, they faded into obscurity, leaving little behind but the phrase, "the Messiah". It is very likely that it was the mystique

44

surrounding these priestly fighting men which was originally responsible for the mystique which came to attach to the term, "the Messiah", and which resulted in its eventual identification with the role of Redeemer which Isaiah had invented.

The Hebrew word, "mashiach", meaning "anointed", originated as an adjective, not a noun, which was applied to certain individuals in Tanach because they were in fact anointed with oil. As Joseph Klausner puts it on page 7 of *The Messianic Idea In Israel*, "In the Holy Scriptures kings, Israelite and foreign, and high priests are described by this word, for all of these were anointed with oil." However, Klausner also notes that in some of the later books of Tanach the word "Mashiach" was used as a noun, and he concludes:

> From these examples we see that the word *Mashiah*, which was originally only another term for "anointed with oil", gradually became a title of honor signifying "chosen", because the act of anointing with oil was a sign of choice and elevation.

Klausner dates this shift in the meaning of the word "Mashiach" from the period following the Babylonian captivity, but he adds that even then the word "Mashiach" in the sense of "Redeemer" did not appear anywhere in Tanach. He believed that it was first used in this sense in the Book of Enoch, which he dated from the time of Herod. But most of the Dead Sea scrolls probably predated Herod, and in view of the political importance of the Qumran sect, who constituted the hard core of the Maccabean party, it would seem that it was they who first popularized the term "Mashiach" in the sense of Redeemer, although not Isaiah's Redeemer..

Why did they choose this particular term and not another? Its main advantage from their point of view is that it could refer equally well to a king or High Priest. The later Maccabees had claimed both titles, and it was only natural for their hard core supporters to assume that their future leader would also somehow combine the two functions. This is probably what was implied in their mind by the phrase, "the Messiah of Aaron and of Israel". At the same time, the term was vague enough to leave open the question of the precise status of the future leader, and this vagueness was in line with the obvious disinclination of the authors of the Dead Sea scrolls to make specific predictions regarding the character of the Redeemer whom they awaited. They were not prophets but warriors, and they wanted a Messiah who could win. What seems to have happened subsequently is that the term, "the Messiah", which they had popularized, came to gradually absorb all of the versions of Redeemer which already existed, and in particular, Isaiah's version. At the same time, it took on new connotations, arising out of the history of the period. This process took a long time, approximately 200 years, from roughly 63 BCE to 135 CE, the date of the end of the so-called "Second Jewish War".

Apocrypha and Pseudepigrapha

The literature that was produced by Jewish writers during this period or shortly before it is commonly called "apocrypha and pseudepigrapha". In terms of understanding the sect that produced the Dead Sea scrolls, the most important text in this literature is undoubtedly the Book of Jubilees, in which the theory and practice of the 364 day solar calendar was set forth at some length. O.S. Wintermute, in his introduction to his translation of the Book of Jubilees in Volume 2 of Charlesworth's anthology, *The Old Testament Pseudepigrapha*, argues that the Book of Jubilees must have been written early in the Maccabean period, prior to 100 BCE. It was certainly written prior to the composition of the Dead Sea scrolls, which draw on it and refer to it. It has a pro-Maccabean character, which Wintermute alludes to on page 44 as follows: "Although the author of Jubilees was one of the spiritual parents of the Qumran sect, he accepted the establishment and was filled with the joy of Maccabean triumphs and hopes for the future." The pro-Maccabean character of the Book of Jubilees is a further indication that the Qumran sect developed out of Maccabean circles and reflected a Maccabean point of view.

The title, "Book of Jubilees", which has been traditionally assigned to this text, is actually something of a misnomer. The Book of Jubilees is basically a revised and condensed version of the Torah. It tells the same story, from the creation of the world to the exodus from Egypt, in much the same way, but with the addition of certain themes

46

which were of particular importance to the author. The main theme which runs throughout concerns the calendar. The book begins with Moses going up to Mount Sinai, where God warns him that the descendants of the children of Israel will stray from the correct path:

> And they will forget all of my laws and all of my commandments and all of my judgments, and they will err concerning new moons, sabbaths, festivals, jubilees, and ordinances.

God then commands the "angel of the presence" to recount the history of the world for Moses "from the first creation until my sanctuary is built in their midst forever and ever." The "sanctuary" in question must have been the Temple, which was clearly central to the world view of the author of the Book of Jubilees.

In the history of the world as recounted in the Book of Jubilees, the issue of the calendar is constantly brought to the fore. Already on the fourth day of creation, a solar calendar is advocated by stating that "the Lord set the sun as a great sign upon the earth for days, sabbaths, months, feast (days), years, sabbaths of years, jubilees, and for all of the (appointed) times of the years". Noah is subsequently told by God to "command the children of Israel so that they shall guard the years in this number, three hundred and sixty-four days, and it will be a complete year." Noah is also warned that advocates of a lunar calendar will attempt to lead Israel astray: "And there will be those who will examine the moon diligently because it will corrupt the (appointed) times and it will advance from year to year ten days." Those who rely on the moon will "set awry the months and the (appointed) times and the sabbaths and the feasts, and they will eat all of the blood with all flesh." But after being forewarned by God, Noah adopts the solar calendar, and since the entire human race is portrayed by the Book of Jubilees, as in the Torah, as descended from Noah, the clear implication is that the 364 day solar calendar is actually the correct calendar for all peoples and not just the children of Israel.

The Book of Jubilees ends with the institution of the festival of Passover and the Sabbath in the time of Moses. The concluding sentence states: "The account of the division of days is finished here." This sentence shows that the real purpose of the entire text was to provide a rationale for the adoption of the 364 day solar calendar. This calendar was tied in with a focus on the seven day week and celebration of the Sabbath, since 364, unlike 365, is divisible by 7. In the perfect world of the Book of Jubilees, there would be 52 Sabbaths every year, and all the festivals and holidays would fall on the same day of the week every year. Concern for the symmetrical celebration of the festivals and Sabbaths was obviously so important for the author of the Book of Jubilees that he arbitrarily reduced the length of the solar year by one day. The length of the solar year was well known by the time the Book of Jubilees was written. The Egyptians had followed a 365 day solar calendar for literally thousands of years by that time, and from at least the 3rd century BCE onwards they had also known about the extra quarter day in the 365 day year. The author of the Book of Jubilees may or may not have known what the Egyptians knew, but it is evident that it was primarily for religious reasons that he insisted on a 364 day year.

What can we infer about the author of the Book of Jubilees from the evidence of the text? It would seem likely that he was part of a faction within the priesthood of the Temple that wished to adopt a new solar calendar as part of a larger program of magnifying the image of the Temple in the eyes of the entire Mediterranean and Middle Eastern world. By the time the Book of Jubilees was written, perhaps around 100 BCE, there were already large Jewish communities, numbering in the hundreds of thousands and even millions, in Turkey, Syria, Egypt, Iraq and Iran. These Jews looked to the Temple in Jerusalem as the center of the Jewish world, and they paid tribute to the Temple, which was under Maccabean control. The greater the power of the Maccabees, the greater the urge of the Maccabean priesthood to amplify its own power. The solar calendar of the Book of Jubilees was evidently intended as a way of doing this. The Temple priesthood and they alone would set the date for holidays and festivals, and these dates would be observed not only in the land of Israel but throughout the Diaspora. It does not seem likely that this program was ever formally adopted by the Temple priesthood during Maccabean times, but it was clearly a popular idea. Exiled from Jerusalem by Salome Alexandra and the Pharisees, the hard core Maccabean faction then reconstituted itself as a sect in the barren wilderness of Qumran and formally adopted the solar calendar as its own..

What follows from this analysis is that there was probably some connection between the solar calendar faction and Alexander Janneus. Adoption of solar calendars is normally a way of glorifying a monarchy. Such was the motive behind the adoption of a solar calendar by the ancient Egyptians, and such too was the motive which led both the Persian and Roman empires to adopt solar calendars in imitation of the Egyptians. Alexander Janneus is known to have had big ambitions. He took over the style and methods of the Hellenistic despots who surrounded the kingdom of Judah and projected himself as their equal or superior. A new Jewish solar calendar promulgated from the Temple in Jerusalem would have fit in perfectly with his approach. Perhaps he did not feel strong enough to openly proclaim the new calendar, but nonetheless encouraged its popularization. Whatever the specific connection may have been, the popularity of the solar calendar scheme should probably be understood as a reflection of the ambitions aroused by his successful conquests.

In addition to the Book of Jubilees, there is also a second "apocryphal" text which mentions the 364 day solar calendar. This is the first Book of Enoch, or "Enoch 1", which is today known only from an Ethiopic translation of a Hebrew or Aramaic original. It most likely dates from the 1st century BCE from the time after the Roman invasions began. Only a few fragments of the Book of Enoch were found at Qumran, whereas there were numerous copies of the Book of Jubilees. This suggests that the Book of Enoch was either less popular with the Qumran sect or else that it was written at a later time when the sect was already beginning to break up. However it bears a closer resemblance to most of the Dead Sea scrolls than does the Book of Jubilees. Its main theme is the same theme that pervades the scrolls: the imminence of a day of judgment on which sinners will be destroyed and the righteous will be exalted. This theme is presented in the form of a series of visions which were supposedly vouchsafed to Enoch, the father of Methuselah in the Book of Genesis. The Book of Genesis states: "Enoch walked with God; then he was no more, for God took him." This cryptic remark made Enoch a likely candidate to receive visions directly from God, which is what happens in the Book of Enoch.

49

Whereas the Book of Jubilees is intended to validate the 364 day solar calendar, the Book of Enoch assumes it. It refers to the calendar only in one section, beginning on page 54 of Volume 1 of Charlesworth's anthology. After describing the progression of the heavenly bodies, the sun, moon and stars, Enoch continues:

> They bring about all the years punctiliously, so that they forever neither gain upon nor fall behind their fixed positions for a single day, but they convert the year with punctilious justice into three hundred sixty-four days.

Whereas the Book of Jubilees warns against reliance on the moon, the Book of Enoch does not even consider the possibility of a lunar calendar, but rather presents all the heavenly bodies as united in their adherence to a solar calendar. The cosmic inevitability of the 364 day calendar is further emphasized by a passage on page 60, where the years, the seasons, the months and the days are said to be controlled by angelic "leaders", who are listed by name in a scheme reminiscent of pagan astrology. The Book of Enoch appears to emanate from a milieu where the 364 day solar calendar was taken for granted and embellished at length. It forms an integral part of Enoch's vision, but it is not a primary concern of the book.

The Book of Enoch is filled with a spirit of hostility to the rich and powerful which is absent from the Book of Jubilees. The following passage, from page 30, describes what will happen on the day of judgment:

> At that moment, kings and rulers shall perish,
> they shall be delivered into the hands of the righteous and
>   holy ones,
> and from thenceforth no one shall be able to induce the Lord
>   of Spirits to show them mercy,
> for their life is annihilated.

In another passage, on page 45, a Messianic figure called the "Elect One" is called in to judge the rich and powerful:

> On the day of judgment, all the kings, the governors, the
> high officials, and the landlords shall see and recognize him

> - how he sits on the throne of his glory, and righteousness is judged before him, and that no nonsensical talk shall be uttered in his presence. Then pain shall come upon them as on a woman in travail with birth pangs - when she is giving birth (the child) enters the mouth of the womb and she suffers from childbearing.

In case anyone missed the point, Enoch goes on to warn the "governors, kings, high officials, and landlords" that "the sword shall abide in their midst" on that day.

Enoch's distrust of all earthly rulers is coupled with an incredibly grandiose image of the coming Redeemer, who is called either the "Elect One" or the "Son of Man". Thus we read on page 35:

> He will become a staff for the righteous ones in order that they may lean on him and not fall. He is the light of the gentiles and he will become the hope of those who are sick in their hearts. All those who dwell upon the earth shall fall and worship before him; they shall glorify, bless, and sing the name of (the Lord of the Spirits) prior to the creation of the world, and for eternity.

Enoch is also told, on page 31: "This Son of Man whom you have seen is the One who would remove the kings and the mighty ones from their comfortable seats and the strong ones from their thrones." He also learns that the "Son of Man" was "concealed from the beginning, and the Most High preserved him in the presence of his power; then he revealed him to the holy and the elect ones." It is evident that it was not a long step from the Book of Enoch to either the Jewish or the Christian conception of "the Messiah".

The Book of Enoch appears to belong to the period when the Jewish monarchy of the Maccabees had already been overthrown by the Romans and Judah was ruled by various Roman puppets. Klausner's theory that it was written during the reign of Herod is very plausible. The author of Enoch must have had some connection with the Qumran sect since he used its solar calendar, but he seems to have lost faith in the possibility of a Maccabean restoration or in the emergence of a Messianic leader with a realistic chance to defeat the Romans. All the same, his conception of the Messiah grew out of the cult of the 364 day solar calendar, which had formed the original basis of the Qumran sect. The whole point of the calendar was to assert the hegemony of the Maccabean priests of the Temple as the ultimate religious authority over a wide constituency that included but was not confined to the approximately 10 million Jews who lived in the eastern Mediterranean region, including the land of Israel, at that time. This was an ambitious program, and the notion of the Messiah as the "light of the gentiles" was encouraged by this ambition. The less Enoch believed in the original Maccabean program, the more he believed in a "Son of Man" or "Elect One" who would one day illuminate the entire world. But at the same time, he integrated the 364 day solar calendar into this program of world illumination by treating this calendar as the expression of vast cosmic forces set in motion by the heavenly bodies and various angelic beings acting on instructions of the "Lord of Spirits" himself.

What basically distinguishes the Book of Enoch from most of the other literature associated with the Qumran sect is the total absence of any thought that the "righteous and holy ones" could achieve their deliverance by their own efforts. Their task is merely to suffer and endure until God chooses to reveal the "Son of Man" and place him upon his throne. There is no final battle, no restoration of the legitimate Jewish monarchy, no set of rules for the elect. All "kings and rulers" are condemned, not merely wicked ones. The Book of Enoch probably reflects a situation in which the Qumran sect was in the process of disintegration as a result of the Roman invasion and the military defeat of the Maccabean faction. The author does not speak as the representative of an organized group but as an isolated individual. This stance is consistent with the choice of Enoch as his spokesman, since Enoch was a obscure figure who was not associated with any particular doctrine or tendency. However the Book of Enoch was sufficiently popular to inspire several later Books of Enoch, commonly known as "Enoch 2" and "Enoch 3", which further developed the theme of Enoch's relationship with God which was the original basis for "Enoch 1".

There is a passage in "Enoch 2" which appears to imply the 364 day solar calendar, but this reference to the calendar seems to have been simply taken over from "Enoch 1" without any particular emphasis or interest. None of the other books of the "apocrypha and pseudepigrapha" refer to the 364 day calendar, suggesting that interest in the calendar did not survive the collapse of the Maccabean cause. And of course, the fact that the calendar would have slipped further and further out of line with the actual solar year as time went by undoubtedly contributed to its decline in popularity. In short, there is every indication that the Qumran sect basically fell apart as hopes for a Maccabean restoration gradually faded during the second half of the 1st century BCE. Its legacy to the Jews of Roman times was the legend of the coming Messiah. This legend, which had its origin in the writings of Isaiah and the prophets, now took deep root due its association with a group of priestly warriors who had formed the hard core of the Maccabean armed forces. The Pharisees continued to await the Messiah of Isaiah, while others looked for the Messiah of Qumran, but in one form or another, the legend of the Messiah became a key component in the Jewish ideology of Roman times. This simple fact was the obvious starting point of the Christian religion.

Christianity

Christianity is first and foremost the doctrine that a certain individual was in fact the expected Messiah of the Jews. There is every reason to assume that this doctrine was founded on the belief of the original followers of that individual that he was the expected Messiah. These followers then transmitted this belief to a man named Saul of Tarsus, later known as the apostle Paul, who in turn created a whole religion around this belief. Leaving aside Saul's religion for the moment, it seems appropriate to first ask: why did the original followers think it so important that Jesus be Christ? Why did they later create a legendary biography of miracles and wonders in order to validate their belief that he was the Messiah? And in particular, precisely what was their relationship, if any, to the religion of the Maccabees?

That some relationship must have existed is strongly suggested by the positive image of Judah the Maccabee in Christian tradition. Yet there is no indication that the original Christians followed a solar calendar or thought of themselves as holy warriors. Nor was it the normal practice in the mainstream Jewish Messianic movement of the first two centuries CE to place such emphasis on whether or not a given individual was "the" Messiah. Only Simon bar Kochba, the leader of the Jewish forces during the "Second Jewish War" of 132-35 CE, was formally hailed as "the" Messiah, and even then bar Kochba did not use this title on his coins. For most Jewish Messianists, "the" Messiah was the Messiah who succeeded. Why did the original followers of Jesus Christ continue to insist that he was "the" Messiah even after he had been defeated?

It seems likely that the explanation has something to do with the Temple. Very possibly the individual later known as Jesus Christ aspired to take charge of the Temple on the basis of the claim that he was "the" Messiah. Belief in this claim then became a common bond holding his followers together after his death. Perhaps they wished to assert some claim to authority over the Temple in his name. But in 70 CE the Temple was destroyed by the Romans, ending the possibility of any form of Jewish authority over it. The descendants of the original followers of Jesus Christ, who became known as Ebionites, maintained themselves as a small sect for some time and then dissolved. They are today forgotten, except as they are pictured in the New Testament, a compilation of Greek language tracts put together by Saul of Tarsus and the Christians. In these tracts, the insistence of the Ebionites that Jesus Christ had been "the" Messiah is given an entirely new significance. It becomes the basis for a pseudo-cannibal ritual in which Christians are enjoined to pretend to eat the flesh and drink the blood of Jesus Christ in order to attain unto eternal life. From the rank of "Messiah", the New Testament promotes Jesus to the rank of "Son of God", the better to enjoin pretending to eat his flesh and drink his blood.

Pretending to eat the flesh and drink the blood of the "Son of God" was a well established custom in Greco-Roman society long before the Christians arose. The original "Son of God" was the baby Dionysos, the son of Zeus according to the mythology of the Orphic mysteries of Greece. According to the Orphics, one day the baby Dionysos was playing with his nurses and the Titans came along, slew him and ate him, thinking thereby to become immortal. Zeus destroyed the Titans with a thunderbolt, but from their remains the human race was born. To attain unto the immortal life inherent in their

54

alleged Titan nature, the Orphics felt it necessary to commemorate the cannibal feast of the Titans with a vegetarian meal of bread and wine, symbolic of the flesh and blood of the baby Dionysos. The Romans took over these rites and popularized them under the name of the cult of Bacchus. Similar rites were then applied by the Greco-Romans to gods from other nations, such as Osiris from Egypt, Adonis from Phoenicia and Attis from Phrygia. Pretending to eat a god in effigy had become a common practice in Greco-Roman society by the time that Christianity arose. The whole claim to fame of Christianity was solely that the Christians could prove that their "Son of God" was an actual person, "the" Messiah in fact, named Jesus. For this they needed the testimony of the Ebionites, whom Paul used for this purpose but otherwise kept at arms length.

The irrelevance of the Ebionites to Paul's Christianity is shown by the fact that there is not one single Christian document in any language other than Greek that emanates from the first three centuries CE. The Ebionites were of course Aramaic speaking, while Paul and his followers spoke Greek. They popularized Christianity in the Greek language communities of Egypt, Syria and Turkey, eventually extending their influence to Greece and Rome. Meanwhile the Ebionites settled in Jordan after 70 CE and had no influence outside of a small circle of Aramaic speaking Jews. The Christians of the 2nd and 3rd centuries CE actually condemned them as "heretics" because they did not approve of pretending to eat the flesh and drink the blood of their dead leader. Their basic doctrines are amply documented by Hans-Joachim Schoeps in *Jewish Christianity*. On page 11, Schoeps sums up the Ebionite attitude towards Jesus as follows:

> The Ebionites saw Jesus as a reformer of the Mosaic law. In particular, he condemned and rejected the sacrificial cult. His messianic mission culminated in the abolition of bloody animal sacrifice and accordingly he annulled the laws which dealt with sacrifice while otherwise remaining loyal to and observant of the Mosaic law.

This is a plausible description of the Ebionite view. It would have put them at odds with the entire Temple priesthood, whose main function was to conduct animal sacrifice, and also to some degree with the

55

Pharisees. This would account for the alienation of the Ebionites from Jewish society and their flight to Jordan. There they disappeared into irrelevance, since the main goal of their dead leader was evidently to preside over the reformed rites of a Temple which ceased to exist after 70 CE.

It would seem that the sectarians of Qumran also wanted to "reform" the rites of the Temple at least so far as the calendar was concerned. But the Ebionite concept of "the" Messiah differed sharply from the Messianic ideology of the priestly warriors of Qumran. It was rather a further extension of the Messiah of Isaiah, whom Isaiah had credited with amazing powers arising from his saintly nature. For the Ebionites and the Christians after them, the claim that Jesus had possessed magic powers was the main basis for their assertion that he was "the" Messiah. This claim was undoubtedly first made by the Ebionites, but the Christians seized on it even more since it fit in perfectly with the additional claim that he was also the "Son of God". So what we have here is a small Messianic movement to "reform" the rites of the Temple which is remembered today solely because a group of ex-Jewish Greek pseudo-cannibals chose the Messiah of this movement as their "Son of God", to be eaten in effigy on a regular basis.

The members of this small Messianic movement resembled the sectarians of Qumran not only because they wished to "reform" the Temple rites but also because of their hostility to the Pharisees. Hostility to the Pharisees is so pervasive in the New Testament that the very term, "Pharisee", has become a byword for hypocrisy and deceit in Christian culture. Perhaps the Ebionites were not quite so antagonistic to the Pharisees as Paul and the Christians, but there must have been some basis for the New Testament image of constant clashes between Jesus and the Pharisees. Yet there is something puzzling about this image, because it was the Pharisees who were the main advocates and popularizers of the Book of Isaiah, which was so central to the Ebionite conception of the Messiah. And in general, Christianity was clearly strongly influenced by the Judaism of the Pharisees, which placed a strong emphasis on the virtue of "hesed", "loving kindness", and was far more pacifistic than the Judaism of the Maccabees. There is nothing in the teachings of Jesus,.as reported in the New Testament, that is inconsistent with Pharisee doctrine. But the Pharisees evidently did not see Jesus as "the" Messiah, and it was most likely for this reason that the Ebionites became hostile to them. This hostility then provided an additional reason to preserve a positive image of the Maccabean tradition, which had also become associated with hostility to the Pharisees during the course of the 1st century BCE.

Somewhere at the core of the link between the religion of the Maccabees and Christianity is the fact that the Maccabees had not only restored the traditional rites of the Temple but consecrated this restoration with a new religious holiday, the festival of Hanukah. Is it merely a coincidence that Hanukah is celebrated on the 25th of Kislev and Christmas is celebrated on the 25th of December? Kislev is the month on the Jewish lunar calendar that most closely approximates December on the Roman solar calendar. Who copied whom here? The Roman solar calendar was not adopted until the time of Julius Caesar, at which point the date of Hanukah had already been fixed for over 100 years. Only after the adoption of Caesar's "Julian calendar" did the Romans begin to celebrate December 25 as a holiday. At first, in the 2nd and 3rd centuries CE it was called "birthday of the sun" and celebrated as the birthday of the various Caesars who claimed to be earthly incarnations of the sun gods "Sol Invictus" or "Mithra". Diocletian, Constantine's predecessor as Caesar, organized huge torchlit parades in his honor as a sun god on December 25. When the Christians took over under Constantine, they seized on December 25 and made it the birthday of Christ instead of Caesar. But why did the Romans think December 25 was the "birthday of the sun" in the first place?

The winter solstice, after all, actually falls closer to December 21. Didn't the Romans know this? If their astronomical information was so good that they were able to design a workable solar calendar complete with a leap year, why did they get the date of the winter solstice wrong by four days? Is it conceivable that they chose the 25th of December as the "birthday of the sun" because it provided a Roman imperialist counter-date and counter-festival to the 25th of Kislev, date of the Jewish "festival of lights"? But this could only be true if Jewish influence in the Roman empire was so strong that the Romans felt the need to counter it. Was this the case? Most conventional histories of Roman antiquity ignore this possibility, preferring to see the rise of Christianity as the inevitable result of the divine qualities of Jesus. But what if the rise of Christianity were merely the culmination of a long history of Jewish influence within the Roman empire? Then the celebration of Christmas on December 25 might appear as a kind of counter-Hanukah, just as Easter is, after all, quite explicitly a counter-Passover. And this Christian counter-Hanukah would appear as the outgrowth of an older counter-Hanukah, the counter-Hanukah of the Roman Caesars, who perhaps celebrated December 25th as their birthday to highlight the fact that it was they who had destroyed the Jewish Temple in Jerusalem.

Lurking somewhere in the background of these speculations is the possibility that Judah the Maccabee became a legendary figure not only for the Jews but for many others as well. For the Jews, it would seem that he was so legendary that even the pacifistic Christians felt the need to accept him. The Pharisees likewise incorporated Hanukah into their tradition and spoke well of Judah the Maccabee. But there was nonetheless a profound difference between the religion of the Maccabees and either Christianity or rabbinic Judaism. Failure to recognize this difference mars the work of the historian Robert Eisenman, who went to great lengths to establish a direct connection between the Maccabees and the Christians. Eisenman believed that James, the brother of Jesus Christ, was the "Teacher of Righteousness" described in the Dead Sea scrolls. This same theory was then disseminated in popular form by Michael Baigent and Richard Leigh in *The Dead Sea Scrolls Deception*. But contrary to the view of Eisenman and his followers, the positive image of Judah the Maccabee in Christian tradition did not derive from an ideological affinity between Maccabean and Christian doctrine but rather from the tremendous prestige of Judah the Maccabee and the key role of the Maccabees in the development of the Messianic ideal, an ideal which the Christians, after their fashion, also shared..

What caused this ideal to assume the form that it finally did was what happened after the Romans arrived in Judah in 63 BCE. The great unreported fact of world history is that there took place, in the 1st and 2nd centuries CE, something analagous to the Holocaust of modern times. The Romans and their Greek allies killed something like 2 or 3 million Jews during this period out of a total Jewish population of approximately 7 million within the boundaries of the so-called "Roman empire". The total number of Jewish casualties reported by Josephus for the "First Jewish War" add up to approximately 1,300,000. The Roman historian Dio Cassius states that 580,000 Jews were killed during the "Second Jewish War". Historians estimate that many hundreds of thousands of Jews were killed by the Romans and Greek during the "Diaspora Revolt" of 115-17 CE. There were close to 1 million Jews in Egypt alone at the start of this period, yet hardly any remaining by the end of the 2nd century CE. The large Jewish communities in Syria and Turkey were likewise decimated. Jews had formed 10% of the total population of the Roman empire and at least 20% of the population of its Middle Eastern portions prior to start of the Roman mass murders. By the end of the 2nd century CE, only 750,000 Jews remained in Judah, home of something like 4 million Jews prior to the Roman onslaught. Most Jews within the Roman empire had been killed or enslaved; most Jews who survived were outside the Roman reach in Iraq, Iran, Yemen, Ethiopia and the mountains of North Africa. The Greco-Roman Holocaust is well documented and has been known to historians for centuries, yet it is almost entirely missing from standard accounts of "classical antiquity".

In its place stands the Christian religion. If it is viewed in the light of the Greco-Roman Holocaust, Christianity appears as above all an extreme case of Holocaust denial. In place of the martyred Jewish nation appears one martyred Jew victimized by, of all people, the Jews themselves. Josephus reports that the Romans crucified literally thousands of Jews outside the walls of Jerusalem during the siege of 70 CE. They then proceeded to destroy the Temple. Isn't it obvious that Christianity, in its own way, symbolized a certain reaction to these facts? It was the reaction of Jews like Paul, who wished to become a part of the Greco-Roman culture that had spawned and glorified the mass murder of the Jewish people. Vespasian and Titus, the Roman generals responsible for the mass murders in the "First Jewish War", became Caesars. Hadrian, the author of the "Second Jewish War", was already a Caesar, and is remembered today as one of the "greatest" of the Roman Caesars. So too is Trajan, under

59

whose rule the massacres of the "Diaspora Revolt" took place. Christianity offered a way to become part of this culture by having your Judaism and eating it too. It arose in the very area where most of the mass murders took place, the land of Israel itself and what are today Egypt, Syria and Turkey. It became popular during the period of the mass murders, and the most obvious reason for its popularity was that it provided a substitute for Judaism in a region where Judaism had become a crime punishable by death. Hadrian actually issued such an edict, and although it was partially rescinded by his successor, conversion to Judaism remained a capital crime under European law right down to modern times.

It is a gross insult to the Jewish people that these facts, which are easily documented and have been known for centuries, are so rigorously excluded from the study of classical antiquity. The more they venerate Jesus, the more they insult us. Even Jewish historians, who are well aware that the Messianic ideal arose from "suffering", are generally reluctant to spell out in appropriate detail the full extent of this "suffering". In addition to the mass murders, the Romans also killed and oppressed Jews throughout the entire period of their rule. The last of the Maccabean kings was crucified by Roman troops under the command of Marc Antony. Many Jews were killed by the Romans during their fighting with the Maccabean forces, which continued off and on for some 20 years after 63 BCE. Tens of thousands of Jews were killed by the Greeks in urban riots in cities like Alexandria and Antioch. This mounting tide of murderousness was directed at the Jewish people by the Greco-Romans with the deliberate intent of bringing to an end all trace of Jewish influence within their "empire". Is it not evident that Christianity had the deliberate intent of frustrating this plan, while at the same time accommodating itself to Greco-Roman culture with its pseudo-cannibal rituals and obsessive anti-Semitism? Christianity was a kind of compromise between the pro-Jewish outlook of one part of Greco-Roman society and the anti-Jewish outlook of another. It preserved the Messianic ideal and sacred texts of the pro-Jewish segment, but encapsulated them in an anti-Jewish narrative which ultimately proved acceptable and even useful to the anti-Jewish segment.

At the root of this entire process was the prestige and authority which the Maccabean High Priests had enjoyed prior to 63 BCE. It was this prestige and authority that was in large part responsible, first for the spread of Jewish influence within the Roman empire, then for the Greco-Roman counter-assault, and ultimately for the Christian compromise. But due to the ferocity of the Greco-Roman counter-assault, not only was the prestige and authority of the Maccabees eventually forgotten, but the religion of the Maccabees also faded from sight, to be replaced in time by the "sects" of modern historiography. It seems abundantly clear that these "sects", including the Ebionite sect that was the starting point of Christianity, were just so many attempts to preserve and validate the Maccabean tradition in the face of the Roman assault. Yet at the same time, all these "sects" necessarily diverged from that tradition due to the failure of the Maccabees to retain control of the Temple after 63 BCE. In order to reconstruct the religion of the Maccabees, the "sects" should be seen as fragments of a shattered whole, whose original unity was predicated on the link between Torah and Temple.

The Torah

Because it became central to rabbinic Judaism, it is easy to lose sight of the fact that the Torah is first and foremost a priestly document. A large part of it is devoted to the duties and responsibilities of the Temple priesthood, and it was essentially the creation of that priesthood. No one knows precisely how and when the Torah was compiled, but it is generally thought that the version which now exists dates from the time of Ezra and Nehemiah, the period of the return from Babylonian exile at the end of the 6th century BCE. The important point is that the Torah was standardized and reproduced in precisely the same form from that time onwards. By the time of the Maccabees, it had acquired the status of the authoritative repository of Jewish law and tradition, and there is every reason to believe that the Maccabees, who came from a priestly family, viewed it in that light.

From a Maccabean point of view, there was therefore a close link between physical control of the Temple and enforcement of the laws of the Torah. And one of the key laws of the Torah was the stipulation, in Chapter 25 of the Book of Leviticus, that land should be restored to its rightful owners, and all slaves set free, in the Year of the Jubilee, the 50th year. In the light of the strong backing which the Maccabees received from the farmers in Judah, it seems likely that they made some effort to enforce the laws of the Jubilee. Both the Greeks and the Romans, on the other hand, were associated with a program of expropriation of the small farmers to make way for large agricultural estates worked by slaves or serfs. In social terms, the Maccabean opposition to Greco-Roman rule could be seen as a revolt of small farmers against a coalition of militaristic landlords and merchants who bought and sold the produce from the large estates of the landlords. There have been many such revolts in world history, but not many have succeeded. The Maccabees attracted attention because they came to power on a radical program, the Torah, and remained in power for approximately 100 years. They had every reason to encourage the spread of the Torah, and there is every reason to believe that their religion was to turn Judah into a Torah state. It was the Torah, after all, on which the rites of the Temple were based, and it was the claim to preside over the rites of the Temple which was the distinctive feature of Maccabean rule.

The relevance of the Torah to the religion of the Maccabees has been obscured by its association with rabbinic Judaism. A large part of rabbinic tradition is derived from sources outside the Torah such as the writings of the prophets or the so-called "Oral Torah", the teachings of the rabbis themselves. But the rabbis rose to prominence as interpreters of the Torah, and so they are seen as representing the Torah point of view in their dispute with the Maccabean kings. Nothing could be further from the truth. The Torah is the story of how and why the land of Israel was given to the Hebrews by God. It was the Maccabees who defended this point of view, while the Pharisees went so far as to ally themselves, first with the Greeks in the time of Alexander Janneus, then with the Romans in 63 BCE, out of hatred for Maccabean rule. The Pharisee party was almost entirely urban, and even the workers in the cities were more closely tied to Greco-Roman rule than were the farmers because so much of the urban economy came to depend on the commerce which the Greco-Romans stimulated. The Pharisees were prepared to make their peace with Greek and

Roman rule so long as the Greco-Romans permitted them the free exercise of their religion. The Temple was part of this religion prior to 70 CE, but not the most important part. The most important part was observing the laws of the Torah, both written and oral, as a code of conduct. The die-hard nationalists were the farmers, who stood to lose their land if the Greeks and Romans remained in power. And since the Torah was their title deed to the land, defense of the Torah, defense of the Temple and defense of the land were undoubtedly all one and the same in their eyes.

After the Roman occupation began in 63 BCE, this unity was gradually undermined. Defense of the Torah came to be primarily associated with the Pharisees, who viewed it as the basis for a code of conduct which was in fact derived in large part from other sources. The priestly party, which came to be known as Sadducees, was purged of its Maccabean leadership and drawn by Herod into the Greco-Roman net of wealth and privilege. Defense of the land ceased to be a practical possibility and was transformed into a utopian hope sustained by Messianic expectations. These were the conditions under which the various "sects" flourished, each perpetuating some aspect of the Maccabean tradition, but none able to reestablish the unity of Temple and Torah which the Maccabees had upheld. Nonetheless it was the memory of Maccabean rule which constituted the foundation on which the various Messianic visions were constructed. Of these visions, the one which was to loom largest in the subsequent history of the Messianic ideal was that of the Zealots.

Chapter Three: The Zealots

Everybody with any sense knows that the Zealots are at the heart of the Messianic tradition. It was they who led the rebellion against Rome, they who were crucified in the tens of thousands by the Romans. The only real issue is: who were the Zealots, and why did they go to war with Rome?

The English word "Zealot" is the term commonly used to provide an English language equivalent to the Hebrew word "Kana". The word has somewhat different connotations in Hebrew than in English. It comes from a root which also carries the meaning of "jealous" or "envious". In modern Hebrew, it can also have the connotation of "fanatic". When used in Tanach in the sense of "zealous", it first appears as a description of Phinehas, a Hebrew priest in the time of Moses who killed a Hebrew man for consorting with a Midianite woman at the moment when the Hebrews were preparing for war with the Midianites. He killed the woman as well, whereupon "the Lord", in Verse 11 of Chapter 25 of the Book of Numbers, tells Moses:

> Phinehas, the son of Eliazar, the son of Aaron the priest, hath turned away my wrath from the children of Israel, in that he was zealous in My stead in the midst of them, that I consumed not the children of Israel in My indignation.

The phrase, "zealous in My stead in the midst of them", has an added meaning in Hebrew, because the word here translated as "zealous" is also applied by Tanach to "God Himself" in the sense of "jealous" or "envious".

God had been planning to send down on a plague on the Hebrews for lusting after pagan deities, but Phinehas, by acting as God would have wished, stayed his wrath. God's well known "jealousy" of other deities was thus the root of the "zeal" of Phinehas. The status of Phinehas as the true executor of God's will was then confirmed by God, who further told Moses, with reference to Phinehas:

> Therefore say, Behold, I give unto him My covenant of peace;

64

And it shall be unto him and unto his seed after him a covenant of an everlasting priesthood; because he was zealous
for his God, and made an atonement for the children of Israel.

Phinehas is also mentioned in the Book of Judges, where he is portrayed as asking God whether or not to go to war "against the children
of Benjamin my brother". God tells him to go to war. In its original
context, therefore, a "Zealot" was a Hebrew who was ready to strike
down other Hebrews in conformance with God's will.

This interpretation is confirmed by the fact that in Tanach, the
term "zealous" was also applied to Elijah, after he killed the prophets
of Baal, and Jehu, who killed the descendants of Ahab. Martin Hengel
on page 151 of *The Zealots* also brings out that the term "zealous" is
used in the first Book of Maccabees with reference to Mattathias, the
father of Judah the Maccabee. Mattathias launched the Maccabean
revolt by killing a Jew who was about to take part in a pagan religious
ritual. The Book of Maccabees says of Mattathias: "He burned with
zeal for the law, as Phinehas did against Zimri, the son of Salu." Like
Phinehas, Mattathias was a priest. However, he did not only kill the
Jew but also the non-Jewish Greek official who was presiding over
the pagan ceremony. It would seem therefore that the association of
"zeal" with Mattathias introduced a subtle shift into the connotations
of the term, which had previously been linked almost exclusively with
the killing of one Hebrew by another on religious grounds. This element was also present in the actions of Mattathias, but what was
remembered about him was primarily the fact that he had struck down
a Greek official. Likewise, the Zealots of the 1st century CE also
attacked other Jews on religious grounds, but what was remembered
about them was primarily the fact that they attacked the Romans.

Hengel's book, *The Zealots*, is undoubtedly the most important
study of the Zealots which has yet been published. Hengel stresses
the religious background of the Zealot movement, an emphasis which
is confirmed by the history of the concept of "zeal" in Jewish literature.
If the term meant anything, it meant opposition to pagan religious practices. It also carried the specific connotation of a readiness to kill
those Jews who took part in such practices and those non-Jews who
induced them to do so. In the context of Roman rule, this meant

65

armed struggle against both the Romans and those Jews who were perceived as imitating them. The concept of "zeal" also carried the implication of inflicting the death penalty through extra-legal means. Neither Phinehas nor any of the later "Zealots" was officially authorized to kill the people whom they killed. They took the law into their own hands in the belief that they were acting in conformance to God's will. Indeed, it is clear that in Jewish tradition God was the original "Zealot", since the term in the sense of "jealous" or "envious" was first applied to him and only subsequently to Phinehas and the others.

But although Hengel's stress on the religious basis of Zealot ideology is clearly justified, his notion of precisely who the Zealots were is open to question. On page 382, Hengel distinguishes five groups described by Josephus who took part in the later stages of the first Jewish rebellion against Rome: the "Sicarii"; the followers of John of Gischala; the followers of Simon bar Giora; the Idumaeans; and the "so-called Zealots", who were linked to the Temple priesthood. Of these five groups, Hengel believes that only the "Sicarii" really merited the title of "Zealots". He thinks they belonged to a highly disciplined underground organization which was founded by Judah of Galilee after the death of Herod and carried on by his sons and grandsons. Yet on Hengel's own showing, the term "Zealot" was also commonly applied to the radical supporters of the Temple priesthood, which is not surprising in view of the fact that both Phinehas and Mattathias had been priests. Moreover, in later Jewish usage, all of the rebels against Rome were frequently described as "Zealots". Hengel himself, on page 66, cites a passage from the Talmud which states: "When the Emperor Vespasian advanced to fight against Jerusalem, the 'Zealots' tried to burn all the supplies with fire." It is unlikely that this passage referred specifically to the "Sicarii", who were mainly concentrated in Jerusalem itself at that time. While the various factions who took part in the rebellion may have differed somewhat in their religious beliefs and practices, they all had one thing in common: a willingness to kill Romans. It was this willingness which defined them as "Zealots" in the eyes of posterity, and there does not seem to be any valid reason for picking and choosing among them who were the truc "Zealots" and who merely the "so-called Zealots".

The original reason why the rebels against Rome came to be

known as "Zealots" is probably that in the early stages of the movement it was more directed against Jewish sympathizers with the Romans than against the Romans themselves. Josephus does not emphasize this side of the story in his account for the obvious reason that Josephus himself was a Jewish sympathizer with Rome. The earliest "Zealots" under Roman rule were probably the Jewish opponents of Herod and his supporters. They concentrated their wrath on the pro-pagan tendencies of the Herodians, and only after the death of Herod and the decline of the Herodian party did they begin to focus their animosity more and more on the Romans themselves. The more they fought the Romans, the more the term "Zealot" came to be associated primarily with anti-Roman sentiment. And since the various "Zealot" factions also fought among themselves, there was ample justification for retaining the original connotations of the term as well. It is also possible that when used by opponents of the "Zealots", the term may have carried connotations of "jealous" or "envious". Most Zealots, after all, came from the poorer classes of Jewish society, while most of their opponents, including Josephus,. came from the rich.

Just what was it in pagan religion that the Zealots so strenuously opposed? The answer goes back to the time of the Habiru revolt against and flight from Pharaoh. The Zealots were above all opposed to the religion of rulers like Pharaoh, which is to say, rulers who defined themselves as gods. That is what Antioches Epiphanes did, and that is what the Caesars did right from the start. Rulers who claimed to be gods also generally claimed the right to treat their subjects like dirt. Accommodation to the religion of such rulers was therefore a clear sign of the acceptance of the division of society into a minority of wealthy oppressors and a majority of impoverished slaves and farm workers. The more worship the Caesars demanded, the more slaves the Romans employed. And just like Antioches Epiphanes, some of the Caesars became enchanted with the idea of having a statue of themselves placed in the Jewish Temple for the Jews to worship. Caligula was about to actually attempt to do this when he was assassinated. Other Caesars encouraged desecration of the Temple by the Roman procurators who ruled over "Judea" after Herod's death. One way or another the Romans were determined to put the Jews in their place and affirm the status of the Caesars as gods by taking control of the Jewish Temple. It was this constant pressure from the Romans that outraged the Zealots and ultimately provoked the Jewish uprising.

Control of the Temple was of course a religious issue, but at the same time it symbolized a whole set of related social, economic, political and cultural issues. The more the Romans pressed for control of the Temple, the more they also pressed to remake Jewish society and culture in their own image. Jewish resistance to this process assumed a religious form, but it also assumed other forms. Bands of armed Jews roamed the countryside in the period leading up to the Jewish uprising. Josephus called them "robbers", and although he undoubtedly exaggerated this side of the picture, it is unlikely that he entirely invented it. Nor is it likely that most members of these armed bands were all that strict in their religious practices. Were they therefore not Zealots? Did they not fight and kill Romans? Did they not defend the Temple? They did, and even more effectively than Hengel's true Zealots the "Sicarii". Even Hengel admits that the strongest fighting force among the last ditch defenders of Jerusalem was that led by Simon bar Giora, which was composed in large part of liberated slaves and "robbers". It was also Simon bar Giora whom the Romans treated as the leader of the insurrection and publicly executed in the Forum to celebrate their victory. Hengel thinks that he made Messianic claims. He also thinks such claims were made by Judah of Galilee and his son or grandson Menachem. Whatever the exact details, there can be little doubt that the Zealot movement was the main reason for the spread of the Messianic ideal on a Mediterranean wide scale during the 1st century CE.

The Jewish Temple, after all, had a Mediterranean wide image. It was just for this reason that the Romans were so determined to control it. Its destruction by the Romans in 70 CE cemented their image as invincible conquerors and assured the rule of the pagan Caesars for several centuries. Is it really just a coincidence that when this rule was finally ended it was replaced by the cult of a crucified Jew? Tens of thousands of Zealots were crucified by the Romans. Simon bar Giora was tortured to death. Christianity was Europe's way of dealing with these memories. Christianity enshrined what it claimed was the authentic Jewish cult of the Messiah in the context of an anti-Jewish fable and narrative. But the Christian version of the Jewish cult of the Messiah is heavily slanted in favor of the Messiah of Isaiah, the Messiah who rules exclusively by the power of the spirit. Such Messiahs did not do well against the Romans. Everyone with any sense realizes that the Zealot version of the Messiah must have been quite different from that of Isaiah. But how different and in what way?

Josephus is not much help here because he was studiously uninterested in the subject of "the Messiah". To read Josephus you would hardly know that the concept even existed in his time. The closest he came to mentioning it, notes Hengel on page 237, is a passage where he lists, as one of the causes of the rebellion, the finding by the Jews of "an ambiguous oracular pronouncement, which had also been found in Holy Scripture, that one man from their country would at that time be given command over the world". This is the closest that Josephus comes to admitting the existence of Messianic beliefs among the rebels. And it is not very likely that such beliefs took the form that Christians imagine, that of waiting for "the" Messiah. For the Zealots, "the" Messiah could only be the leader who succeeded in defeating the Romans. Victorious leaders were anointed, which made them "Messiah", with or without the "the". So the key to understanding the Zealot concept of the Messiah is understanding the Zealot concept of victory. How on earth could they have hoped to defeat the mighty Romans? Were they just acting out of desperation, or did they actually have a strategy to win?

The Temple

Victory for the Zealots meant first and foremost physical control of the Temple. This control was challenged by the Romans in the name of paganism in general and Caesar worship in particular. In the name of what did the Zealots resist the Roman challenge? The Temple was the physical center around which the entire Jewish people revolved. Its preservation in Jewish hands was a symbol of sovereignty, a symbol that Jewish law remained the law of the land. But the Maccabean revival of Jewish sovereignty had been cut short by the crucifixion of the last of the Maccabean kings by the Romans and his replacement by the Roman puppet king, Herod. Herod's death many decades later ushered in a period in which no widely recognized form of Jewish sovereignty still existed. The High Priests were seen as Roman puppets, as were the remnants of the Herodian party. Judah had ceased to exist as a political entity and the Roman province of "Judea" over which Herod had ruled had been broken up into smaller units. Among whom was zeal for the Law most likely to arise at this time? Among priests no doubt, and priests of the Temple in particular.

Phinehas and Mattathias had been priests, and they were the defining figures of the Zealot concept in Jewish tradition. The Qumran sect had been led by priests, and its ideas clearly had a major impact on the ideology of the Zealots. Zealot usage of the term, "the Messiah", was very likely derived from the Qumran sect. Priests had a strong motive to defend Jewish control of the Temple since their livelihood was bound up with it. And in the absence of legitimate High Priests, they had every reason to remember that God had said to Phinehas that he would form "a covenant of an everlasting priesthood" with him and his "seed" because he had acted as God would have acted. His "seed" could easily be interpreted to mean his spiritual descendants. This was undoubtedly the root meaning of the Zealot concept in the Roman period. The founders of the Zealot movement had every reason to view themselves as the spiritual descendants of Phinehas, forming an "everlasting priesthood" based on armed opposition to Greco-Roman paganism. At first, they may have directed this opposition primarily against pagan influence among Jews, but at some point they came to focus more on the Romans. Hengel's belief that the people whom the Romans called "Sicarii" (meaning "assassins") were actually Zealots is most likely correct. But there is no reason to assume that these people were all disciples of Judah of Galilee. It is far more likely that their original leadership came from the priesthood in and around the Temple. This was the group that had the strongest motive to promote the idea that the Messiah "would be given command over the world", as Josephus put it. The notion of such "command" was but a metaphorical extension of the power which the priesthood already exercised as the official guardians of a Temple renowned thoughout a large part of the Mediterranean and Middle

Eastern world

A key detail in this context is the fact that Herod had rebuilt and greatly enlarged the Temple around the year 20 BCE. Josephus describes the rebuilding process at great length in Book 15, Chapter 11 of *Jewish Antiquities*. He says that the reason Herod gave for enlarging the Temple was that it was not yet as large as the Temple built by Solomon and destroyed by the Babylonians. According to Josephus, Herod stated:

> Our fathers, indeed, when they were returned from Babylon, built this temple to God Almighty, yet does it want sixty cubits of its height; for so much did that first temple which Solomon built exceed this temple; nor let anyone condemn our fathers for their negligence or want of piety herein, for it was not their fault that the temple was no higher; for they were Cyrus, and Darius the son of Hystaspes, who determined the measures for its rebuilding; and it has been by reason of the subjection of those fathers of ours to them and to their posterity, and after them to the Macedonians, that they had not the opportunity to follow the original model of this pious edifice, nor could raise it to its ancient altitude.

Herod went on to suggest that the Romans were willing to let him enlarge the Temple, the implication being that Roman rule was more favorable to the Jews than Persian or Greek rule. Josephus further relates that after the necessary building materials had been assembled, "the temple itself was built by the priests in a year and six months, upon which all the people were full of joy." They had feared that Herod would tear down the Temple and not rebuild it, but in fact the Temple as reconstructed on Herod's orders was one of the largest and most impressive public buildings in the ancient world.

Herod's rebuilding of the Temple fit in with the program of Julius and Augustus Caesar, which was to treat Judaism as a "legal religion" while integrating "Judea" into the Roman empire with the aid of Herod. However, starting with Tiberius, the successor to Augustus, the Roman Caesars became increasingly hostile to Judaism as a religion and to "Judea" as a political entity. The main reason for their hostility was undoubtedly the spread of Judaism within the Greco-Roman world. And the spread of Judaism was in turn linked to the prestige of the

Temple, to whose upkeep each Jew throughout the world was expected to contribute. The weaker the political authority of the Jews became after the death of Herod, the more the Temple appeared as the sole surviving expression of Jewish sovereignty. It was for precisely this reason that the Caesars were gradually drawn to the idea of either converting it to Caesar worship or destroying it altogether. The priests of the Temple, who were the ones who actually rebuilt it according to Josephus, were the natural leaders of the Jewish opposition to the Greco-Roman pagan offensive. Even though the leading priestly families may have been corrupted and bought off by the Herodian party, the priests as a group necessarily remained dedicated to Jewish tradition, on which their own authority rested.

Most historians identify the priestly party in Judah during the 1st century CE with the group whom Josephus called, in Greek, "Sadducees". According to Josephus, there were three main parties in Judah at that time: the Pharisees, the Sadducees and the Essenes. The term, "Sadducee", is generally thought to derive from the Hebrew expression, "Zadokim", meaning Zadokites, descendants or followers of the first High Priest of the Temple, Zadok. However, Josephus does not explicitly link the Sadducees with the priests. What he says about them is that whereas the Pharisees believed in fate and the afterlife, the Sadducees did not. He continues as follows, in Book 2, Chapter 8 of *The Jewish War*:

> Moreover, the Pharisees are friendly to one another, and are for the exercise of concord, and regard for the public; but the behavior of the Sadducees one towards another is in some degree wild, and their conversation with those that are not of their own party is as barbarous as if they were strangers to them. And this is what I had to say concerning the philosophic sects among the Jews.

It seems clear that Josephus did not like the Sadducees, who probably did not like him either. Their disbelief in an afterlife might appear to indicate an irreligious attitude on their part, but it is a striking fact that the concept of an afterlife is almost entirely absent from Tanach. The Sadducees probably viewed it as a new fangled innovation introduced by the Pharisees, as indeed it was. Most historians see them as a conservative, wealthy, priestly faction, but this image does not fit well with the terms "wild" and "barbarous" which Josephus applied to them.

As a rule, whenever Josephus bad mouths a group, this is a sure sign that they were hostile to the Romans. However, Josephus states in Book 13, Chapter 10 of *Jewish Antiquities* that "the Sadducees are able to persuade none but the rich, and have not the populace obsequious to them, but the Pharisees have the multitude on their side." The difficulty of understanding the Sadducees is further compounded by the fact that the term was rarely if ever used in the literature of the period apart from the works of Josephus and a few references in the New Testament to "Pharisees and Sadducees". As Donald Akenson notes in *Surpassing Wonder*, there is no text from this period that can be reliably ascribed to a Sadducean author. Akenson concludes, on page 196:

> Granted, we can accept that a group which contemporaries called "the Sadducees" existed up to 70 C.E. However, since they left no identifiable text, no contemporary avowals of membership, and only post -Temple reports of their beliefs (and these by their rivals) "Sadducee" is best taken as a flexible, umbrella term for an undefined group of religious conservatives.

The thing is, the Zealots were also "religious conservatives". Assuming that the term "Sadducee" referred in a general way to the priestly party, the Zealots might well have constituted its radical wing, whose attitude led Josephus to characterize all the Sadducees as "wild" and "barbarous". This wing was probably based on the less wealthy priests, and in particular those associated with the Temple guard.

Eleazar, the commander of the Temple guard, played a leading role in the rebellion against the Romans. It is likely that anti-Roman sentiment had been building for decades among the Temple guards, since they would have been directly involved in any clash between the Romans and the Jews regarding authority over the Temple. Another relevant detail in this context is that the first time Josephus actually uses the term, "Zealots", in *The Jewish War* is to describe a group of rebels who seized control of the Temple and attempted to appoint a new High Priest from their own ranks. According to Josephus, in Book 4, Chapter 3 of *The Jewish War*, this particular group of rebels became known as Zealots "as if they were zealous in good undertakings, and were not rather zealous in the worst actions, and extravagant in them beyond the example of others." It would seem, however, that what actually marked them as "Zealots" was the fact that they wanted to control the Temple in a manner that Josephus regarded as illegal and inappropriate. This would suggest that the term, "Zealot", had come to denote not only religious zeal in general but also in particular religious zeal relating to control of the Temple. The people most likely to have manifested such zeal in the decades leading up to the rebellion were the temple guards and lower ranking priests of the Temple. Having ceased to respect the authority of the "legitimate" High Priests, who were generally Roman puppets, it was only natural for them to gravitate in the direction of an underground movement aimed at the overthrow of Roman rule, the elimination of paganism and the establishment of a new Jewish state headed by a Messianic High Priest.

It is possible that some light on the origins of the Zealots may be cast by one of the Dead Sea scrolls commonly known as the "Temple Scroll". No one is sure exactly when it was written, but several indications point to the later decades of the reign of Herod. For one thing, with reference to the appointment of a king of Judah, it contains the admonition, on page 485 of *The Dead Sea Scrolls: A New Translation*: "You must not put a foreigner over you, he who is not one of your brethren." Herod was widely viewed as a "foreigner" because he came from a family of Idumean converts to Judaism. For another thing, it is concerned with the rebuilding of the Temple, an issue which was brought to the fore by Herod. The "Temple Scroll" envisions the construction of a huge new temple complex, one which would be roughly equivalent in size to the entire city of Jerusalem as it then existed. It is as if the author of the scroll wished to outdo Herod, at least in thought, and create a new Temple even bigger and better than his. The author must have belonged to the Qumran sect, for he used the characteristic solar calendar of this sect and even added new holidays and festivals. Yet if the "Temple Scroll" dates from the time of Herod, as appears likely, it can also be seen as an early expression of the Zealot point of view, which undoubtedly grew out of the ideology of the Qumran sect to a very considerable extent.

As the editors of *The Dead Sea Scrolls: A New Translation* note in their introduction to the "Temple Scroll", it was intended as a kind of "new Deuteronomy", a new set of laws for the Jewish people transmitted by God to an unidentified "new Moses". The new laws resembled the old but differed on several key points. In particular, several key features of Deuteronomy are omitted. The editors list these, concluding as follows on page 459:

> Another striking series of omissions occurs whenever the biblical book mentions foreigners or sojourners. The *Temple Scroll* omits all such passages. Its author conceives of an Israel in which no foreigner lives within the boundaries of the land - none at all. Thus his new law needed no regulations for such groups. This extreme xenophobia appears in a number of the Dead Sea Scrolls.

What the editors characterize as "extreme xenophobia" could also be characterized as "zeal", since the essence of "zeal" was precisely the repudiation of paganism. It would seem that the stronger pagan influence in the land of Israel became under Herod and his successors, the more opposition to paganism became a distinguishing feature of the emerging Zealot movement.

Another feature of the "Temple Scroll" that appears to resemble Zealot ideology is its image of the nation of Judah as consisting of concentric circles of holiness radiating out from the Holy of Holies of the Temple and eventually encompassing the entire land. From this point of view, physical control of the Temple was the key to religious devotion everywhere. And since Jews in the Diaspora were also expected to contribute to the upkeep of the Temple, the concentric circles of holiness could also be envisaged as extending beyond the land of Israel to encompass a wider area. Herod's enlargement and improvement of the Temple must have stimulated just such an enlargement of the Zealot frame of vision. The author of the "Temple Scroll" was concerned only with the land of Israel, but the later Zealots could easily have seen themselves as engaged in a life and death struggle with Rome not only for Jewish independence but also for the spread of the Jewish way of life throughout the surrounding region. This attitude would have fit in well with the growing tendency in the 1st century CE to view "the Messiah" not merely as the future ruler of Judah but also as a source of inspiration for the entire world.

Viewed in this light, physical control of the Temple can be seen as the keystone of a strategy that aimed not just at the defeat of the Roman invaders but the export of Jewish religious ideals beyond the boundaries of the land of Israel. This was, after all, the only strategy that had even a remote chance of success. Given the size of the Roman empire and its huge, well equipped army, there is no way that the Zealots could have hoped to overthrow Roman rule in the land of Israel without also attacking the foundations of Roman rule in general. And the Zealot emphasis on opposition to paganism did in fact attack those foundations. Taken together with the existence of a large Jewish Diaspora throughout the Roman world numbering millions of people, the Zealot repudiation of Caesar worship did constitute a certain threat to Roman rule in general. It was no doubt for just this reason that the Romans became increasingly determined to either impose Caesar worship on the Temple or destroy it entirely. The Temple thus became, both in theory and in practice, the focal point of a struggle which was couched primarily in religious terms but also had broad social, political, economic and cultural implications. And it was undoubtedly because of these implications that the Zealot movement gradually broadened from its original core of priestly fanatics to embrace a large part of the Jewish people.

Robbers

The term most commonly used by Josephus to describe the rebels against Rome was neither "Zealots" nor "Sicarii" but "robbers". His constant implication was that most of the rebels had no real ideology but were motivated solely by the thought of personal gain and feelings of resentment and hostility towards those more wealthy and better educated than themselves. He saw these "robbers" as a threat not only to the Romans but also to the Jewish upper classes, to which he himself belonged. He believed that the Jewish upper classes made a fatal mistake by launching the rebellion, thereby permitting the "robbers" to come to power and wreak untold havoc before they were finally and justly put down by the Romans. Josephus did not express these ideas in a subtle and indirect way, but openly, repeatedly and forcefully. He thus confronted all subsequent historians with the difficult task of deciding to what extent his image of the "robbers" was determined by his obvious bias and to what extent it actually corresponded with the facts.

Doron Mendels, in an article appearing in Charlesworth's anthology, *The Messiah*, surveys the historical literature bearing on this point. He sees two main schools of thought. The first, chiefly represented by Hengel, believes that "most groups fighting the Romans acted together in one way or another, and that they had a common messianic vision." The second maintains that "all the groups terrorizing the Romans acted separately and that few, if any had a messianic ideology." Mendels himself managed to uphold both conflicting schools of thought on two successive pages of his article. On page 263 he states: "Judging from the Essene writings and the Pseudepigrapha, which antedate 70 C.E., messianism is not of major importance." This is followed by the statement, on page 264, that "messianism in its biblical connotation no doubt permeated all classes, groups, and sects." By "biblical connotation" Mendels probably meant the Book of Isaiah, although he does not say so explicitly.

A good example of the second school of thought is *The Ruling Class of Judaea*, published in 1987 by Martin Goodman. Goodman treats the works of Josephus as if they were holy writ. He does upgrade the "robbers" to the status of "bandits", but otherwise he is in perfect agreement with the contention of Josephus that the majority of rebels were animated by nothing more than the desire for plunder and class hatred of the rich. As he puts it on page 226: "The bandits who thus provided much of the manpower for the civil war seem to have chosen the faction they joined for reasons common to all mercenaries, the prospect of pay and booty and the likelihood of success." This characterization is in turn based on Goodman's acceptance of the position of Josephus that the in-fighting among the rebels was caused by various ambitious and unscrupulous leaders stirring up the ignorant masses to plunder the rich. Hengel, on the other hand, believed that conflicts among the rebel factions were caused by ideological differences, a contention which was in turn based on his belief that all the rebels were motivated to one extent or another by religious convictions. The bottom line is that Hengel sympathized with the rebels while Goodman did not. It would seem that the degree to which different historians believe Josephus depends in large measure on whether or not they agree with his overall attitude towards the rebellion.

The most likely conclusion is that both sides are right. There is little reason to doubt that many of the rebels were in fact animated by class hatred and did in fact seek to plunder the rich. There is also little reason to doubt that religious ideology did play a major role in stimulating mass opposition to the Romans and their crypto-pagan Jewish sympathizers. The majority of the rebels are probably best understood neither as dangerous bandits nor as starry eyed idealists but as a bit of both. The important question is: what was the mediating term between these two extremes? The obvious answer is: the egalitarian bent of Jewish religious tradition.

Jewish egalitarianism originated with the Habiru and was perpetuated in Jewish religious literature. The writings of the prophets are filled with denunciations of the rich and expressions of concern for the poor. In the Book of Micah we read, in Chapter 2:

> Woe to them that devise iniquity
> And work evil upon their beds!
> When the morning is light, they execute it,
> Because it is in the power of their hand.
> And they covet fields, and seize them;
> And houses, and take them away;
> Thus they oppress a man and his house,
> Even a man and his heritage.

Similar statements are also found throughout the Dead Sea scrolls, the Apocrypha and Pseudepigrapha. The first Book of Enoch, on page 75 of Volume 1 of Charlesworth's anthology, states:

> Woe unto you, O rich people!
> For you have put your trust in your wealth.
> You shall ooze out of your riches,
> For you do not remember the Most High.

In the days of your affluence, you committed oppression,
you have become ready for death, and for the day of darkness and the day of great judgment.

In the light of this literature, plunder of the rich by the rebels against Rome could just as well be regarded as an act of religious piety as one of criminal transgression.

That Josephus saw the matter differently is above all an indication of how strongly he had been influenced by Greco-Roman pagan culture. There is not a trace in the writings of Josephus of an affirmation or even an awareness of the egalitarian component in Jewish religious tradition. He did not so much deny as ignore it, but we may safely assume that the rebels against Rome were well aware of the many condemnations of the rich and warnings of the advent of a day of judgment that fill the pages of Jewish religious literature. The concept of the Messiah also reflected this egalitarian tradition, because one of the key features of this concept was that the Messiah could come from any class of Jewish society. Neither Moses, nor Joshua, nor David, nor Judah the Maccabee - who were the main prototypes of the Messianic ideal in Jewish tradition - had come from a family with a strong hereditary claim to rule over the land of Israel. It is true that Isaiah stated that the future Redeemer would be a descendant of David, but this qualification was not included in most literary expressions of the Messianic ideal in Roman times. Moreover, as the Christians proved, just about anyone could be alleged to be a descendant of David some 1000 years after his time. In practice, the Messianic ideal therefore encouraged rebel leaders from the lower classes of Jewish society to think of themselves as potential leaders of Jewish society as a whole.

It is also likely that the rebels against Rome were aware to some extent of the many examples in earlier Jewish history of the formation of armed bands in the countryside in the name of the defense of the Jewish religion and the rights of the poor. Judah the Maccabee had organized just such a movement of armed guerrilla bands, as had David before him. The founders of Jewish tradition, the Habiru, consisted entirely of armed bands of runaway slaves and other fugitives. Many inscriptions dating from the 2nd millenium BCE refer specifically to the Habiru as "bandits". An echo of these accusations is preserved in the word "Hebrew", which comes from a Hebrew root which can have the meaning of "cross over" but also "transgress" or "violate". The term "Habiru" probably also had these same connotations. It is significant that in the Torah, the only time the Hebrews are actually called "Hebrews" is when a non-Hebrew is speaking about them. Otherwise the Hebrews are invariably called "the sons of Israel", a term which they obviously much preferred to that of "Habiru". Many Habiru probably really were bandits, but under the influence of Moses and the Habiru fugitives from Egypt, they became theocrats instead. In later centuries, whenever Jewish tradition and independence seemed in danger, there was a built-in tendency to revert to the Habiru model, flee to the countryside and form armed bands.

Hengel makes a similar point on page 336 of *The Zealots* where he notes that the tactics of the Zealots resembled those of "the young David, the early Maccabeans, Athronges and his followers and finally those who took part in the revolt of Bar Kochba." Hengel also brings out how often the actions of the "robbers" expressed a broader social vision and not just the desire for plunder. He notes on page 133 that one of the first acts of the rebels led by Judah of Galilee was to destroy the archive where the record of land ownership was kept "presumably because the distribution of land at that time bore no relationship to the ideal dispensation which was prescribed in Lev 25 and Deut 15 and which was at the same time also in accordance with their own social aims." Simon bar Giora was more radical still, forming his army in large part from slaves whom his followers had liberated. R.A. Horsley, in an article appearing in Charlesowrth's anthology, *The Messiah*, states:

> By far the most important "messianic" movement of the first century was that focused on Simon bar Giora, who eventually became the principal political-military commander in Jerusalem during the Jewish Revolt and whom the Romans ceremonially executed as, in effect, the king of the Jews.

It would be foolish to imagine that the followers of Simon bar Giora never robbed anyone, but "robbers" or even "bandits" do not appear to be really apt terms for the Messianic movement to which they belonged.

What remains unclear is the precise nature of the relationship between the hard core of priestly "Zealots" and the mass movement of armed "robbers". What makes this relationship particularly difficult to understand is that the only people whom Josephus specifically called "Zealots" in *The Jewish War* actually bore a much closer resemblance to his stereotype of "robbers". In fact, he began by calling them "robbers" and only switched over to "Zealots" after they had seized control of the Temple. He says that they were "robbers that came out of the country, and came into the city" and then "undertook to dispose of the high priesthood by casting lots for it, whereas, as we have said already, it was to descend by succession in a family." It is very likely that Josephus called them "Zealots" in a sarcastic vein, as if to say: "look, priestly fanatics, this is what your fanaticism has led to". For Josephus, "Zealot" had to be regarded as inherently a prestigious term because of its association with Phinehas and Elijah, but the "Zealots" who seized control of the Temple during the revolt were, in his eyes, merely low class country bumpkins without any standing or legitimacy. Conversely, Josephus was probably reluctant to admit the existence of a movement of priestly "Zealots", since this would confer a higher status on the rebellion than he wished to assign to it.

The one thing that can be safely concluded from the account of Josephus is that there existed various doctrines among the rebels as to the correct organization of worship in the Temple. According to Josephus, the "Zealots" who wanted to cast lots for the office of High Priest claimed they were acting in accordance with an ancient tradition, whose validity was challenged by some priests and affirmed by others. Since there was no longer any priestly family whose claim to the office of High Priest was widely recognized, different factions were at liberty to invent different doctrines as to who should preside over the rites of the Temple. Some rebel leaders may have aspired to the title of High Priest, others to that of king, still others to a Messianic combination of the two. The only firm basis of unity among them was the belief that the Temple must remain in Jewish hands and that the Romans must be expelled from the land of Israel. This belief had both social and religious implications, and it is reasonable to assume that the "robbers" stressed the former while the priestly Zealots stressed the latter. As to the precise connection and balance of forces between these two tendencies, Josephus is not a reliable guide and there is no other.

There can be little doubt, however, that the Messianic ideal was an important aspect of both tendencies. It was found both in religious literature and popular culture. Contrary to the assertion of Mendels that "messianism is not of major importance" in the Pseudepigrapha, it forms the central theme of one of the most popular "pseudepigraphal" works, the "Psalms of Solomon". Written in the late 1st century BCE or early 1st century CE, the "Psalms of Solomon" describes a situation in which Jerusalem has been seized and despoiled by "the gentiles". The people of Israel have become "sinners", but deliverance, on page 667 of Volume 2 of Charlesworth's anthology, is at hand:

> See, Lord, and raise up for them their king,
>   the son of David, to rule over your servant Israel
>   in the time known to you, O God.
> Undergird him with the strength to destroy the unrighteous rulers,
>   to purge Jerusalem from gentiles
>   who trample her to destruction;
>   in wisdom and righteousness to drive out
>   the sinners from the inheritance.

And the psalm continues:

> And he will be a righteous king over them, taught by God.
> There will be no unrighteousness among them in his days,
>   for all shall be holy,
>   and their king shall be the Lord Messiah.

The psalm also indicates that after the Messiah appears to lead the people of Israel, "the alien and the foreigner will no longer live near them", suggesting a close connection between the doctrines of the "Psalms of Solomon" and those of the "Temple Scroll" and the Zealots. The "Psalms of Solomon" also reveals a concern with social issues, stating: "Happy is (the person) whom God remembers with a moderate sufficiency; for if one is excessively rich, he sins."

Moreover, although Josephus displays a massive disinterest in Jewish Messianic ideology, he does discuss a doctrine which may well be his version of Jewish Messianism. This is the "fourth philosophy", which he describes in Book 18, Chapter 1 of *Jewish Antiquities*. After having previously stated in *The Jewish War* that there were three philosophies among the Jews, those of the Pharisees, Sadducees and Essenes, Josephus adds a fourth, which he ascribes to the teachings of Judah of Galilee, "who excited a fourth philosophic sect among us, and had a great many followers therein, filled our civil government with disturbances then, and laid the foundations of our future miseries, by this system of philosophy, which we were before unacquainted with, concerning which I will discourse a little, and this the rather because the infection which spread from there among the younger sort, who were zealous for it, brought the public to destruction." The expression, "who were zealous for it", conveys a strong hint that this was the philosophy of the Zealots.

Josephus set forth the teachings of the "fourth philosophy" as follows:

> But of the fourth sect of Jewish philosophy, Judas the Galilean was the author. These men agree in all other things with the Pharisaic notions, but they have an inviolable attachment to liberty, and say that God is to be their only Ruler and Lord. They also do not count the cost of dying any kinds of death, nor indeed do they heed the deaths of their relations and friends, nor can any such fear make them call any man lord.

It was this passage which led Hengel to conclude that Judah of Galilee was the founder of the Zealot movement. As he rightly noted, the contention that "God is to be their only Ruler and Lord" carried the obvious implication that neither Caesar nor any ruler appointed by the Romans could be their legitimate king. And although Josephus did not say so, the belief in God as the sole legitimate ruler could easily coexist with and motivate a belief in the Messiah as God's surrogate ruler on earth.

Judah of Galilee was the son of Hezekiah, a "robber captain" according to Josephus, who had led a rebellion in Galilee against Herod and been executed on his orders. Hengel points out that Herod's execution of Hezekiah led to protests from the members of the Sanhedrin in Jerusalem, suggesting that Hezekiah was "a man of rank and influence". Judah of Galilee led the opposition to the Roman census in 6 CE, and his sons and grandsons played leading roles in the revolt against Rome. It was therefore plausible for Hengel to assume that the rebel dynasty founded by Hezekiah constituted the real leadership of the Zealots and that the "fourth philosophy" which Josephus ascribed to Judah of Galilee was the true Zealot doctrine. But there are a number of problems with this interpretation. In the first place, Hezekiah and his descendants were not priests, and the Zealot doctrine was rooted in priestly tradition. In the second place, the Zealot movement was centered around the Temple and Jerusalem, whereas the movement led by Hezekiah and Judah of Galilee was centered in Galilee. On the other hand, Josephus does convey the strong impression that Judah of Galilee was the founder of a doctrine which was popular among the Zealots. The most likely conclusion is that the emerging Zealot movement drew on both priestly sources and also the example of Judah of Galilee, fusing both into a Messianic ideology which gained increasingly wide acceptance in Jewish circles in the decades leading up to the revolt against Rome.

That Judah of Galilee actually thought of himself as enunciating a "philosophy" is highly doubtful. "Philosophy" was not a Jewish but a Greco-Roman concept which Josephus assigned to the various Jewish parties because he was writing for a Greco-Roman audience. The important point about Judah of Galilee, and Hezekiah before him, was not their "philosophy" but the fact that they put their ideas into practice, actually taking up arms, first against Herod, then against the Romans. It was the power of the example which they set which undoubtedly spurred the growth of the Zealot movement. The notion that God was the only legitimate ruler was in some sense fundamental to all forms of Judaism, but at first it was only a radical fringe which carried this notion to the point of open rebellion. Perhaps the priestly Zealots were also inspired by this example. In any case, there was no lack of attempts by the later rebels against Rome to set up earthly rulers who claimed to rule in the name of God. The "fourth philosophy" seems to have been a code word devised by Josephus to describe Jewish Messianism. He probably viewed Judah of Galilee as the first of the would-be Messiahs, a view echoed by Hengel. Later would-be Messiahs could then be described as disciples of the "fourth philosophy", but what they were really imitating was the attempt to overthrow Roman rule and institute Jewish rule.

Eschatology

It seems evident that an anti-Roman movement arose among the Jewish people during the course of the 1st century CE that was led by people called Zealots. This term probably originally referred to the members of a priestly-led secret society who carried out attacks on the Romans and who were known to the Romans as "Sicarii". By extension it came to refer to all of the Jewish rebels against Roman rule. The Zealot movement aimed at the expulsion of the Romans and the establishment of a Jewish state headed by an awaited charismatic leader who would become either the High Priest or king or both. The awaited leader would institute a regime of perfect justice based on authentic Jewish tradition. The good guys would be rewarded, the bad guys would be punished. Land lost through debt would be restored, slaves would be set free. The example of a free Judah would inspire movements for liberation throughout the Roman world.

What remains to be determined is the relationship between this set of beliefs and another set of beliefs which clustered around it but was not identical to it. These are the beliefs generally labelled "eschatological" or "apocalyptical". Such beliefs were founded on the expectation of a "Day of Judgment", at which time human history as commonly understood would come to an end. The dead would rise, sinners would be punished with eternal damnation and the righteous would ascend to a world of heavenly glory. The "Kingdom of God" would be revealed for all to see, complete with a vast hierarchy of angels and demons, saints and sinners.

These beliefs were to some extent rooted in Jewish tradition but did not become widespread until the Greco-Roman period. In the writings of the prophets, there are scattered references to a coming "Day of the Lord". In the Book of Joel, Chapter 4, we read:

> Multitude, multitudes in the valley of decision!
> For the day of the Lord is near in the valley of decision.
> The sun and the moon are become black,
> And the stars withdraw their shining.

However, Joel and the other prophets were somewhat vague as to precisely what was supposed to happen at this time. The only reference to the resurrection of the dead that appears in Tanach is to be found in the "Book of Daniel", which is thought to have been written in the 2nd century BCE. It was probably around this time that "eschatological" and "apocalyptic" works first became popular. There are a number of such works to be found among the "Apocrypha" and "Pseudepigrapha", and similar themes are also present in the Dead Sea scrolls.

As some authors have pointed out, belief in the Messiah was not a necessary component of "eschatology" and is not found in many "eschatological" works. God, after all, was thought to be perfectly capable of handling a "Day of Judgment" all by himself. Mowinckel, on page 280 of *He That Cometh*, puts it this way:

> In proportion as the main emphasis came to be laid on the religious aspect of the future hope, on the kingly rule of Yahweh, there would be little or no room for the Messianic king, in whom, after all, at least in the traditional belief, earthly and human features predominated.

On the other hand, some eschatological works, like the first "Book of Enoch", did include a Messianic figure alongside God. What seems probable is that as belief in the coming of the Messiah became an increasingly important element in Jewish culture, this belief tended to find its way into an "eschatological" literature that had, for the most part, initially dispensed with it.

What role did the believers in the "end of days" play in the Zealot movement? Josephus describes a number of preachers, or "false prophets" as he calls them, who tried to stir up the people against the Romans during the period leading up to the rebellion. Thus, in Book 2, Chapter 13 of *The Jewish War*, after denouncing the "Sicarii", he states:

> There was also another body of wicked men gotten together, not so impure in their actions, but more wicked in their intentions, which laid waste the happy state of the city no less than did these murderers. These were such men as deceived

and deluded the people under pretense of divine inspiration, but were for procuring innovations and changes of the
government; and these prevailed with the multitude to act
like madmen, and went before them into the wilderness, as
pretending that God would there show them the signals of
liberty. But Felix thought this procedure was to be the beginning of a revolt; so he sent some horsemen and footmen
both armed, who destroyed a great number of them.

It is reasonable to assume that expectations of an impending "Day of
Judgment" played an integral role in such disturbances. On the other
hand, Josephus nowhere suggests that the "false prophets" were among
the leaders of the revolt itself. It would appear that believers in the
"end of days" were generally supportive of the revolt but not central to
its strategy and tactics.

The point about "apocalyptic" thinking is that it was based on a
certain pessimism about the prospects of salvation in this life. The
more believers in the "end of days" stressed the prevalence of iniquity
and sin in this life, the greater the gap they saw between ordinary
human history and the coming "Kingdom of God". It is significant that
the two "Apocryphal" works in which anti-Roman sentiment is most
clearly fused with "eschatological" and Messianic beliefs were both
written after, not before, the destruction of the Temple in 70 CE.
These are the second "Apocalypse of Baruch" and the fourth "Book
of Ezra". Both are thought to date from around 100 CE. In the
second "Apocalypse of Baruch", the coming of the Messiah is but a
prelude to the end of time. We read on page 631 of Volume 1 of
Charlesworth's anthology:

And it will happen after these things when the time of the
appearance of the Anointed One has been fulfilled and he
returns with glory, that then all who sleep in hope of him will
rise. And it will happen at that time that those treasuries will
be opened in which the number of the souls of the righteous
were kept, and they will go out and the multitudes of the
souls will appear together, in one assemblage, of one mind.
And the first ones will enjoy themselves and the last ones
will not be sad. For they know that the time has come of
which it is said that it is the end of times. But the souls of the
wicked will the more waste away when they shall see all

these things. For they know that their torment has come and
that their perditions have arrived.

Such prophecies were undoubtedly also made before the destruction
of the Temple, but they seem to have become more frequent once any
realistic hope for the liberation of Judah from the Romans had been
smashed. This suggests that the believers in the "end of days" were
also somewhat less optimistic than the hard core Zealots about the
prospects of a military victory over the Romans even before the destruction of the Temple.

Moreover, the Zealots regarded themselves as traditionalists,
but the belief in the "end of days" was not really a traditional Jewish
belief. It had entered Judaism mainly through the influence of the
Pharisees, who justified their adoption of it through the doctrine of the
"oral Torah". According to the Pharisees, alongside the written Torah
there also existed an oral Torah, consisting of teachings which had
been handed down by word of mouth since the time of Moses but
were not written down until much later. The Sadducees explicitly
repudiated the doctrine of the oral Torah and also the belief in the
immortality of the soul which went along with it. Most "eschatological"
works maintained that there was little or nothing that anyone could do
to either advance or retard the "Day of Judgment". It would come
when God in his infinite wisdom intended it to come and not a moment
sooner or later. This stance did not mesh well with the activist bent of
the Zealots. The belief in the "end of days" was nonetheless a popular
doctrine, but one which was probably not all that central to Zealot
ideology.

Outside of the land of Israel, however, the belief in the "end of
days" had a wide resonance. This is because it was associated both
with the Pharisees, who were far and away the most influential Jewish
faction in the Diaspora, and also Zoroastrianism, which had been the
official religion of the Persian empire. Persian rule had been overthrown by the Greeks but Zoroastrian teachings were still popular
throughout the eastern Mediterranean region. In rabbinic literature,
there are a number of statements to the effect that you will know when
the days of Messiah are at hand when you see a Persian (or Parthian)
horse tied to a tree in the land of Israel. The Parthians were a no-

madic people who had expelled the Greeks from Iran in the 2nd century BCE and subsequently fought a number of wars with the Romans for control of the Middle East. The rabbis looked to the Persians and/or Parthians as allies against the Romans, and they were also undoubtedly aware of the close resemblance between their own teachings and those of the Zoroastrians on the subject of "eschatology". Somewhere at the heart of the symbiosis between Jewish and Zoroastrian versions of the "end of days" was also the memory that it was Cyrus, the founder of the Persian empire, who had given permission to the Jews in Babylon to return to the land of Israel and build the second Temple.

Unfortunately for the rebels against Rome, Nero signed a peace treaty with the Parthians in 63 CE, only a few years before the outbreak of the revolt. This treaty remained in force until 113 CE, at which time the Roman Caesar Trajan launched an invasion of Parthian territory in Turkey and Iraq. The Roman invasion of Iraq was accompanied by massacres of the Jews living there, which in turn touched off a widespread uprising of Jews in the eastern Mediterranean region known as the "Diaspora Revolt" of 115-17 CE. Had this revolt taken place at the same time as the Zealot uprising, both rebellions would undoubtedly have had a much better chance of success. And if the Parthians had also been at war with Rome at the same time, the chances of success would have been even further improved. What these considerations suggest is that the Zealot strategy, although doomed to failure, was not entirely unrealistic. It was based on concentric circles of Jewish influence, just like the "Temple Scroll" had suggested, radiating out from a central core of priestly Zealots to a wider circle of dispossesed farmers to an even wider circle of Judeo-Zoroastrian true believers enjoying the support of many millions of people throughout the eastern Mediterranean region. Unfortunately, the Zealots did not have the means or perhaps even the inclination to coordinate the movement of these concentric circles and bring them all into motion at one and the same time. Their focus did not extend much beyond the land of Israel, and even there it was largely centered around Jerusalem and the Temple. They ended up forced into a defensive position, and the Romans excelled at conquering defensive positions.

Defeat did not entirely eliminate the Zealots, but it brought the believers in "eschatology" to the fore. In the fourth "Book of Ezra", the destruction of Rome is predicted, but not by the hand of man. On page 548 of Volume 1 of Charlesworth's anthology, Ezra receives a vision in which Rome is likened to a multi-headed eagle:

> And I looked, and behold, the eagle flew with his wings to reign over the earth and over those who dwell in it. And I saw how all things under heaven were subjected to him, and no one spoke against him, not even one creature that was on the earth.

But soon the eagle hears the voice of a lion, who is actually "the Messiah", speaking on behalf of "the Most High":

> And you have judged the earth, but not with truth; for you have afflicted the meek and injured the peaceable; you have hated those who tell the truth, and have loved liars; you have destroyed the dwellings of those who brought forth fruit, and have laid low the walls of those who did you no harm.

The verdict follows:

> Therefore you will surely disappear, you eagle, and your terrifying wings, and your most evil little wings, and your malicious heads, and your most evil talons, and your whole worthless body, so that the whole earth, freed from your violence, may be refreshed and relieved, and may hope for the judgment and mercy of him who made it.

The spirit of the revolt against Rome lived on in such writings, but the actual destruction of the eagle was left solely in the hands of "the Most High" and "the Messiah whom the Most High has kept until the end of days". Ezra kept asking when that time would come, and the answer he kept getting was: don't hold your breath.

Works such as the "Apocalypse of Baruch" or "Book of Ezra" are also indicative of a little noticed trend that emerged during the period of some 60 years that elapsed between the destruction of the Temple and the start of the Jewish uprising against Rome led by Simon bar Kochba. This was the convergence of Zealot and Pharisee ideology. This convergence culminated in the famous scene where rabbi Akiva, the leading rabbinical authority of his day, hailed Simon bar Kochba as "King Messiah". It is far from clear that Simon bar Kochba was actually all that concerned whether or not he was called "the Messiah". But it must have been a big deal for rabbi Akiva and his followers, for whom the word "Messiah" undoubtedly had strong "eschatological" associations. Akiva died a martyr's death at the hands of the Romans, and it is significant that in later rabbinic tradition, although bar Kochba came to be viewed as a "false Messiah", Akiva himself remained a venerated figure.

Martyrdom

There can be little doubt that the main reason for the convergence of Zealot and Pharisee ideology was the large number of Jews murdered by the Romans during the so-called "First Jewish War" of 66-73 CE. Jews were murdered not only in the land of Israel but also elsewhere, especially in Syria, where the passage of the Roman army was accompanied by mass murders in the city of Antioch. These crimes were accompanied by the destruction of the Temple, the devastation of the land and the sale of many Jews into slavery. Vespasian and his son Titus, the Roman commanders responsible for the mass murders, were hailed successively as Caesars. It was as if Hitler had won and been crowned ruler of a "New World Order". These events chastened the Zealots but also convinced the Pharisees that they had no future under Roman rule. The movement led by Simon bar Kochba was therefore more united, but probably smaller, than the movement eventually led by Simon bar Giora. Both men died a martyr's death, Simon bar Kochba in battle, Simon bar Giora in the Roman Forum.

Isn't it an astonishing coincidence that during this same period of time there should emerge a mass religious movement among the peoples of the eastern Mediterranean region that venerated the figure of a crucified Jew, preserved the Hebrew "Scriptures" in a Greek language format and made innumerable Greek language copies of various "apocryphal" and "pseudepigraphal" works originally written by Jews in Hebrew or Aramaic? You would think that historians of classical antiquity would at least have the decency to notice this coincidence, but with few exceptions none do. To read their scholarly works, you would never guess that the Roman mass murders and destruction of the Temple had even the slightest impact on anything or anybody apart from the Jews themselves. The so-called "Jewish Wars" are generally passed off in a few sentences, or a paragraph or two at best, in the midst of an endless recitation of other wars, other conquests. The rise of Christianity can then be treated as first and foremost the result of the miraculous powers of Jesus Christ and secondarily perhaps as associated with the spread of the "mystery religions" in general. The thought that it might have anything to do with the memory of literally millions of martyred Jews has been more or less rigorously excluded from the European mind for some 2000 years now. Yet it is necessary to accept this thought in order to achieve any kind of realistic understanding of the origins of the Messianic ideal.

Such an understanding has been subverted by the polemical needs of Christianity. For the Christians, the Messianic ideal has to be above all something which Messiahs are expected to conform to. In this way they feel they can prove that Jesus Christ was "the" Messiah, since they can point out all the ways that the New Testament asserts his conformance with that ideal. They pretend not to imagine that anyone could suspect that the New Testament was designed with just this purpose in mind. But in real life it is highly unlikely that most Zealot leaders were all that concerned whether or not they conformed to a literary ideal. Their main concern was to win. For them the Messianic ideal was a code word for victory. From this point of view, the notion of a defeated Messiah is absurd. But the Christians were people who had ceased to believe in the victory of the Jews and had come to believe in the victory of Jewish values instead. Christianity was their way of preaching these values in a non-Jewish and even anti-Jewish form. To this end they took the Messiah of Isaiah and transformed him into a literary figure who had supposedly been scorned, rejected and condemned by the Jews of his day and who had ordered his followers to eat him in effigy shortly before he died. Using Jesus to distance themselves from the Jews, the Christians could then draw on Jewish literary tradition and the teachings attributed to Jesus to lecture the Greco-Romans regarding their lack of ethical behavior.

Christianity is thus a religion with two souls, one pro-Jewish, the other anti-Jewish. Where Christians differ is in which side they tend to emphasize. One side needs the Messiah as an item of sacramental consumption; the other needs the Messiah as the exemplar of a radical agitator. Neither seems to understand that the Messianic ideal became as important as it did because of the real life martyrdom of literally millions of Jews at the hands of the Romans. Total Jewish dead in the period of some 70 years between 66 and 135 CE must have been at least 2 million. Was this simple fact not the root cause of the growing popularity of a cult of a crucified Jew during this same period? Of course it was. But that is not a fact that the Christians are interested in. The fact they want is: who was the real Jesus? So let us search for the real Jesus, the better to understand how the literary Jesus was born.

Chapter Four: The Real Jesus

The main obstacle to the recognition of the real Jesus is the systematic intent of the New Testament to separate Jesus from the Jews. This intent is in turn a reflection of the well documented desire of the early Christians to also separate themselves from the Jews. Various motives have been alleged for this desire, but if we bear in mind the fact that millions of Jews were being murdered during the same period as the early Christian church was taking shape, the most pressing motive for the Christian refusal to be lumped together with the Jews can readily be discerned.

This refusal is manifested throughout the New Testament in all the ways that first Jesus and then Paul are constantly shown in conflict with some Jewish faction or group. The "Pharisees and Sadducees" are the chief culprits, followed closely by the Zealots. As many scholars have noted, the name "Judas Iscariot" is the Greek form of a name that would appear in English as "Judah Sicarius", meaning "Judah the Zealot". Jews never appear as positive figures in the New Testament unless they are followers of Jesus or part of some anonymous "common people" and not identified with any specific Jewish faction or group. All this is intended to make first John the Baptist and then Jesus Christ and then Paul appear as the authors of a novel, unprecedented, uniquely wonderful non-Jewish path to salvation that had previously not been available. In this way, the New Testament creates a huge barrier in the way of attempting to identify Jesus Christ with any particular Jewish sect or tendency apart from that founded by John the Baptist.

As historians have recognized for some 150 years now, the key to finding the real Jesus is placing him correctly within the spectrum of Jewish organizations and ideologies which existed at that time. This recognition has given rise to a large literature devoted to such themes as "Jesus the Zealot" or "Jesus the Essene". What needs to be remembered here is that all four "gospels" were written, in Greek, many decades after the events which they purport to recount. They were written by the followers of Saint Paul, a quarrelsome individual who did not get along well with the original followers of Jesus Christ. No one knows or will ever know precisely how much accurate history the "gospels" recorded and how much sheer fable they invented. But of one thing we can be fairly certain: Jesus Christ must have claimed to be the Messiah.

To be sure, many scholars have questioned this assumption. Israel Knohl notes on page 2 of *The Messiah Before Jesus* that the "main tendency" of New Testament scholarship for the past 100 years has entailed "denying the historical reality of Jesus' claim to messiahship". But this claim is so central to Christianity that it is highly unlikely that it was invented by Paul and his followers. It may be that Jesus and his followers used some term other than "Messiah" to designate the awaited Redeemer described by Isaiah and others, but there is every reason to assume that the belief in Jesus Christ as "the Messiah" started with his original followers and was based on the words and actions of Jesus himself. So if we want to situate Jesus within the spectrum of the Jewish tendencies of his day, the obvious point of departure is among groups for whom the concept of the Messiah was particularly important. As we have seen, such groups were invariably those who were dissatisfied with the way the Temple was being run. Jesus too expresses this dissatisfaction in the New Testament. On behalf of which Messianic group or tendency might he have been expressing such views?

The Essenes

The most likely candidates are undoubtedly the Essenes. But precisely who were the Essenes? This question has been hotly debated by scholars for some time now due to the discovery of the Dead Sea scrolls.

Prior to the discovery of the scrolls, the Essenes were known only through lengthy descriptions of them in the works of Josephus and also brief references to them by the Roman writer Pliny and the Jewish writer Philo. Pliny said they lived by the shores of the Dead Sea, so when the scrolls were found near the shores of the Dead Sea, most scholars immediately concluded that they must have been written by the Essenes. Gradually dissenting voices appeared, and in recent decades the identification of the Essenes as the authors of the

Dead Sea scrolls has been challenged or questioned by many leading scholars of the period.

Norman Golb reviews the evidence and the history of the debate in his penetrating study, *Who Wrote The Dead Sea Scrolls?* Golb concludes that it is unlikely that the buildings at Qumran were an Essene monastery or that the Essenes wrote the majority of the Dead Sea scrolls. For one thing, most of the scrolls appear to date from the mid 1st century BCE, while all the literary references to the Essenes date from the middle or late 1st century CE, at least 100 years later. Pliny's description of the Essenes was written after the destruction of the Temple in 70 CE and conveyed the impression that they were living by the Dead Sea at that time. Qumran, which Golb believed to be a fortress, had been overrun and destroyed by the Romans around 68 CE. Josephus, whose description of the Essenes was based on their activities prior to 70 CE, made no reference to them living by the Dead Sea but instead stated that they had branches in various cities and towns.

Moreover, although there are definite points of similarity between the doctrines of the Essenes as described by Josephus and the doctrines espoused in the Dead Sea scrolls, there are also clear cut differences. Josephus spoke well of the Essenes, a sure sign that he did not regard them as anti-Roman. In fact, Josephus specifically stated, in Book 2, Chapter 8 of *The Jewish War*, that each candidate for membership in the Essenes was compelled to swear "that he will ever show faithfulness to all men, and especially to those in authority, because no one obtains the government without God's assistance". The attitude of the authors of the Dead Sea scrolls towards rulers of whom they did not approve was quite different; it resembled that of the Zealots, not that of the Essenes. Such rulers were condemned as illegitimate, and the faithful were exhorted to prepare to do battle with them. As Golb notes on page 378:

> In scrolls where a messianic figure acts as a deliverer, he often appears to be identified as the "Prince of the Congregation". His main role is to lead the troops of Israel into battle against the nations and restore its national glory.

There is not a word in the writings of Josephus to suggest that the

Essenes held similar views, and it is unlikely that he would have praised them as he did had they in fact held such views.

According to Josephus, the Essenes believed in the immortality of the soul and dedicated themselves to a life of piety and righteousness in the hope of reward in the future life. To this end they pooled their property and lived according to a strict code of conduct. Most although not all frowned on marriage and thought celibacy more conducive to holiness. Particularly revealing is the following passage, from Book 18, Chapter 2 of *Jewish Antiquities*:

> The doctrine of the Essenes is this: That all things are best ascribed to God. They teach the immortality of souls, and esteem that the rewards of righteousness are to be earnestly striven for; and when they send what they have dedicated to God into the temple, they do not offer sacrifices because they have more pure offerings of their own; on which account they are excluded from the common court of the temple, but offer their sacrifices themselves; yet is their course of life better than that of other men; and they entirely bind themselves to husbandry.

The important point here is that the Essenes were evidently embroiled in some controversy over the performance of sacrifices in the Temple "on which account they are excluded from the common court of the temple". So we have here a group of Jews that was not anti-Roman, that considered themselves more virtuous than other Jewish groups and that was involved in a controversy over the rites of the Temple. All these indications point strongly in the direction of the Essenes as the main group from which the doctrines of Jesus Christ were derived.

Although Josephus did not explicitly say so, Essene acceptance of Roman rule was consistent with their heavy emphasis on the doctrine of the immortality of the soul. Josephus describes their beliefs as follows, in Book 2, Chapter 8 of *The Jewish War*:

> For their doctrine is this, that bodies are corruptible, and that the matter they are made of is not permanent; but that the souls are immortal, and continue forever; and that they come out of the most subtle air, and are united to their bodies as to prisons, into which they are drawn by a certain

natural enticement; but that when they are set free from the bounds of the flesh, they then, as released from a long bondage, rejoice and mount upward.

Josephus adds:

And this is like the opinions of the Greeks, that good souls have their habitations beyond the ocean, in a region that is neither oppressed with storms of rain or snow, or with intense heat, but that this place is such as is refreshed by the gentle breathing of a west wind, that is perpetually blowing from the ocean; while they allot to bad souls a dark and tempestuous den, full of never-ceasing punishments.

The stronger the belief in a future life for the "good souls", the less the need to fight the Romans in the here and now. It is also significant that Josephus makes no reference to Essene belief in a stormy "Day of Judgment" accompanied by the resurrection of the dead - which was the main image of the "end of days" in Jewish tradition - but instead goes out of his way to stress the similarity between Essene ideas of immortality and those of the Greeks.

He took up this same theme in *Jewish Antiquities*, stating, in Book 18, Chapter 2, that the Greeks whom the Essenes most resembled were "those Dacae who are called *Polistae*", meaning "dwellers in cities". The group to whom Josephus referred were Pythagoreans, and the doctrines of the Essenes did in fact resemble those of the Pythagoreans in many ways. The Pythagoreans also believed in the immortality of the soul, also had strict regulations, also held themselves to be a spiritual elite. However, the Pythagoreans tended to meddle in politics, while the Essenes give every appearance of having held themselves aloof from politics and concentrated on religion. It is easy to imagine a young Essene steeped in the imagery of the Book of Isaiah who came to believe that he had a divine mission to do whatever it was in the Temple that the Essenes wanted done. It is easy to imagine him gathering a small band of followers and trying and failing to have his way. It is also easy to imagine his followers refusing to admit defeat and elevating the Essene belief in the heavenly ascent of the soul after death to the status of the legend of the resurrection of Jesus. What is less easy to imagine is precisely why Jesus and his followers attached such importance to the claim that he was "the Messiah".

The belief in "the Messiah" was, after all, not a necessary part of "eschatology", and there is no direct evidence that the Essenes did in fact hold such a belief. Josephus gives no hint that they did, and although he may have suppressed this information, the fact that he spoke so well of them suggests that he did not regard them as convinced Messianists. Messianism in his eyes was a dangerous doctrine, asssociated with the rebels against Rome and the Zealots. Also, it was not a Greek doctrine, and Josephus seems to have been impressed by the points of resemblance between the teachings of the Essenes and those of the Greek philosophers. On the other hand, the Essenes were undoubtedly familiar with the many Messianic prophecies in Jewish literature, and some among them must have endorsed these beliefs. What seems unlikely is that the Essenes as a group - and they were intensely group-minded - adhered to the belief in the coming of "the Messiah". So although he probably came from an Essene background, Jesus Christ most likely split off from the Essenes at some point and developed his own doctrine, one which stressed his Messianic vocation more strongly than the Essenes would have approved of.

In so doing he would have resembled the various "false prophets" whom Josephus describes as having tried to stir up the people in the decades preceding the revolt against Rome. This raises the question of why Josephus did not mention Jesus Christ as one of these "false prophets". The Christian copyists who preserved the works of Josephus had the same question, and they eventually inserted a reference to Jesus Christ into the Old Slavonic version of *The Jewish War*. The fact that Josephus did not mention Jesus obviously disturbed them, as well it should, for it suggests the possibility that the Jesus Christ of the New Testament never actually existed and was entirely a literary creation. A number of modern writers have in fact upheld this theory, including Arnold Rothstein in *The Jesus Idea* and Harold Leidner in *The Fabrication Of The Christ Myth*. But although the Jesus Christ of the New Testament is undoubtedly in large part a literary creation, it does not seem plausible that he was invented from scratch. Since Paul did not get along well with the original followers of Jesus Christ, and since there are numerous indications of tension between him and them in The Acts of the Apostles in the New Testament, it would seem that the only reason the New Testament shows them any respect at all is because they were able to testify to the fact that Jesus Christ had really lived and also to the alleged fact that he had worked many miracles and risen from the dead. Even so, the "gospel" narratives tend to look down on them, while Paul is the sole hero of the rest of the New Testament.

But if Jesus Christ was a real person, why did Josephus ignore him? The only plausible explanation of this contradiction is that the movement which Jesus led was too small and insignificant to be well enough remembered for Josephus to include it in his writings. This conclusion is consistent with the view that the Messianic ambitions of Jesus did not represent official Essene doctrine and were not supported by the Essenes as a group. Josephus was born around the time that Jesus died and therefore could only have learned of him through other sources, which were evidently not numerous. The New Testament says that Jesus had twelve followers, and although the number twelve was probably chosen because of its association with the twelve tribes of Israel, it is unlikely that the actual number was very different. It is entirely possible that the leader of a small group of religious dissidents might have been condemned by the Temple authorities and executed by the Romans without anyone except his original followers paying much attention. The "false prophets" whom Josephus does mention had thousands of followers, and although the New Testament strives to give the impression that Jesus was admired by the common people, there is no particular reason to believe that this was so. If all the talk of great miracles and gaping throngs is discounted, we are left with a small band of religious enthusiasts that probably resembled many other such small bands and would have been entirely forgotten had not Paul chanced upon the remnants of the group in Jerusalem and decided to make Jesus the focal point of a new mystery religion.

The fact that some or all of the members of this group came from Essene backgrounds might have been a big plus in Paul's eyes. Although Paul must have been able to speak Aramaic in order to communicate with the original followers of Jesus Christ, Greek was his primary language and all of his letters in the New Testament were written in Greek. His followers too were exclusively Greek speaking; indeed, every single surviving Christian document written prior to the 4th century CE was written in Greek. Since Josephus made such a big point of the resemblance between the "philosophy" of the Essenes and that of the Greeks, it seems likely that Paul would have felt more at home among former Essenes than he did among, for example, Pharisees, whose attitude towards Greek culture was not very positive. It is perhaps for this reason that the Essenes are nowhere mentioned in the New Testament. The New Testament never refers to any Jewish group except to speak badly of them, and Paul and his followers evidently felt that they were not in a position to speak badly of the Essenes, from whose teachings much of Christian doctrine seems to have been derived.

Particularly reminiscent of Christian beliefs were the Essene teachings regarding sex and property. Josephus states in Book 2, Chapter 8 of *The Jewish War*: "These Essenes reject pleasures as an evil, but esteem continence, and the conquest over our passions, to be virtue." He goes on to say that the Essenes were "despisers of riches" and continues as follows:

> Nor is there anyone to be found among them who has more than another; for it is a law among them, that those who come to them must let what they have be common to the whole order, inasmuch that among them all there is no appearance of poverty, or excess of riches, but every one's possessions are intermingled with every other's possessions; and so there is, as it were, one patrimony among all the brothers.

Josephus also depicts them meeting together for a communal supper after they have "clothed themselves in white veils" and bathed "in cold water". Some have theorized that the Christian rite of baptism was derived from this practice, but it is more likely that the Christians borrowed this rite from the Pharisees, who used it as a rite of initiation for female converts in place of the circumcision which was expected of male converts. In any case, there is little which Josephus has to say about the Essenes which could not also be applied to the early Christians.

The only area where a clear difference appears concerns the question of adherence to Jewish law. The Essenes did not question the validity of Jewish law but, to the contrary, followed it even more strictly than the Pharisees or Zealots. However, there is little or no reason to believe that Jesus Christ and his original followers rejected Jewish law. There is every indication that the Christian repudiation of Jewish law was an innovation introduced by Paul and his followers, who no doubt found adherence to Jewish law to be a major obstacle in the way of their assimilation to Greco-Roman culture and society. Jesus and his original followers were not concerned with becoming Greeks or Romans and therefore had no reason to abrogate Jewish law. They seem to have wished to live in much the same way as did the other Essenes, but for some reason or other they had a grievance relating to the Temple that was more intense or extreme than that felt by the Essenes as a group. It must have been this grievance that led Jesus Christ to regard himself as "the Messiah" and therefore entitled to alter the rites of the Temple in some manner. What could this grievance have been, and why did it matter so much?

Sacrifice

Different historians have answered this question differently. There exist at least three distinct secular schools of thought on the subject of the Messianic vocation of Jesus Christ, which are in turn based on three different ways of looking at Christianity as a religion.

The most popular and the least plausible theory is based on the concept of Jesus the Zealot. According to this view, Jesus Christ was really a Jewish revolutionary whose anti-Establishment rhetoric was later toned down and modified by Paul and the Hellenistic Christians. This theory has a long history in Christian "heretical" circles, but its scholarly exposition has been largely the work of 20th century English Marxists and radical Protestants. Archibald Robertson, a Marxist writer, published *The Origins of Christianity* in 1954. He argued on page 93 that Christianity originated as "a revolutionary movement led first by John the Baptist and then by Jesus the Nazoraean, and aimed at the overthrow of Roman and Herodian rule in Palestine".

Similar views were then put forward by such writers as S.G.F. Brandon in *Jesus and the Zealots* and Hyam Maccoby in *Revolution in Judaea*. In one way or another, all the writers of this school argue that Jesus Christ was actually the leader of a popular movement to seize control of the Temple and proclaim a new Jewish state much as the Zealots tried to do some 30 years later. His Messianic vocation would thus appear as a natural outgrowth of his revolutionary ambitions.

Despite its wide appeal in radical Christian circles, this theory is inconsistent with the known facts. In the first place, if Jesus Christ had in fact led a large popular movement, Josephus would have taken notice of it, but he did not. In the second place, the followers of Jesus Christ, who became known as Ebionites, did not act like anti-Roman revolutionaries but instead fled from Jerusalem at the time of the first "Jewish War" and established themselves in Jordan. In the third place, it is highly unlikely that Paul, who prided himself on his status as a Greek-speaking Roman citizen, would have chosen an anti-Roman revolutionary as the hero of his new mystery religion. Nor is there anything substantial in the New Testament or other early Christian writings which suggests adherence to a Zealot ideology of armed struggle against the Romans aimed at the establishment of a new Jewish state. To the contrary, early Christian literature is filled with denunciations of violence of any kind and condemnation of the Jews as unworthy of a state of their own. It is undoubtedly true that Paul was less of a social critic than Jesus, but it is simply not plausible that a religion which accepted Greco-Roman rule should have been founded on a movement intended to overthrow it.

A more plausible but less popular theory is that advanced by many Jewish writers on the subject of Christianity, particulary Joseph Klausner (in *Jesus of Nazareth* and *From Jesus To Paul*) and David Flusser (in *Judaism and the Origins of Christianity*). This might be called the theory of Jesus the Pharisee. While recognizing the Essene component in the teachings of Jesus, such writers tend to draw attention to the many points of resemblance between those teachings and those of the Pharisees. Flusser puts it this way, on page 169:

> There are two roots of Jesus' teaching: his basic ethical doc-

trines stem from the Pharisaic stock, but very often we find Essene influence in his doctrines, primarily in the field of social approach.

Indeed, Flusser goes so far as to argue, on page 510, that Jesus derived his Messianic vocation at least in part from Hillel, the most famous of the early Pharisees, whom Flusser believes had an "exalted" self-concept. Flusser states:

> It is well known that Jesus accepted various aspects of Hillel's moral theology. Thus it is more than probable that Jesus' exalted self-awareness was influenced by Hillel's views about himself.

Be that as it may, it does seem probable that Messianic thinking was more popular among the Pharisees than among the Essenes, and therefore it is at least conceivable that it was Pharisee influence which led Jesus to adopt a Messianic self-concept.

Such a conclusion seems inconsistent with the New Testament image of constant conflict between Jesus and the Pharisees, but it could be that this image was largely the creation of Paul and his followers and did not reflect the actual facts. However, the Ebionites also did not get along with the Pharisees, nor is the resemblance between the doctrines of the Pharisees and those of Jesus in the New Testament quite so close as Flusser asserts. On balance it would seem that although the New Testament undoubtedly exaggerates the antagonism between Jesus and the Pharisees, some degree of tension between them did exist. What the New Testament conceals is the large area of agreement between the two. Jewish historians like Klausner and Flusser deserve credit for bringing out this point, which has now been largely accepted by Christian scholars as well. But although the rabbis were fond of Messianic literature, there are no recorded examples of established Pharisee leaders attempting to project themselves as Messiahs. An organizational connection between Jesus and the Pharisees therefore appears highly improbable. Pharisee teachings may have influenced his Messianic self-concept, but his need to declare himself "the Messiah" cannot be plausibly ascribed to Pharisee influence.

There remains a third possibility, admirably developed by Schoeps in *Jewish Christianity*. According to Schoeps, the Ebionites were vegetarians, and they claimed to derive their vegetarianism from Jesus himself, who had intended to abolish animal sacrifice in the Temple while otherwise preserving Jewish law in its entirety. As Schoeps puts it on page 99: "The Ebionites required abstinence from meat, and this was apparently related to their rejection of the bloodshed involved in animal sacrifice." Moreover, since Josephus specifically states that the Essenes did eat meat, a decision of Jesus to become a vegetarian would fully account for the lack of organizational connection between him and the Essenes. It would also explain why his activities might have been viewed with horror by the priests of the Temple and why they might have wanted him executed. The big problem with this theory, which is otherwise so plausible, is that if Jesus was really executed as a vegetarian and foe of animal sacrifice, some echo of this fact ought to appear in the doctrines of Paul and the later Christians. But although Christianity undoubtedly does have what might be called a vegetarian propensity, there is nothing in the New Testament to indicate that the early Christians were required to abstain from meat altogether. On the other hand, it could be that Jesus really did object to animal sacrifice in the Temple without necessarily advocating vegetarianism. There are numerous passages in the writings of the prophets indicating an ambivalent or hostile attitude towards the practice of animal sacrifice in the Temple. Jesus may well have expressed a similar attitude, and the failure of the New Testament to report this could have been due to the fact that the "gospels" were composed only after the destruction of the Temple in 70 CE, after which the whole issue of what went on in the Temple became essentially irrelevant.

Particularly significant is the presence of a denunciation of animal sacrifice in the Book of Isaiah, the main source of the later Christian delineation of the Messianic ideal. The very first chapter of this book ascribes the following views to "the Lord":

> To what purpose is the multitude of your sacrifices unto
>   Me?
> Saith the Lord;
> I am full of the burnt-offerings of rams,

And the fat of fed beasts;
And I delight not in the blood
Of bullocks, or of lambs, or of he-goats.

And a few lines later, "the Lord" also declares, with evident reference to animal sacrifice:

Your hands are full of blood.
Wash you, make you clean,
Put away the evil of your doings
From before Mine eyes,
Cease to do evil;
Learn to do well;
Seek justice, relieve the oppressed,
Judge the fatherless, plead for the widow.

It is easy to imagine a young Essene reading these lines and deciding that he was called upon to abolish animal sacrifice in the Temple. This is all the more likely in that the Essenes are known to have had a difference with the way the rites of the Temple were conducted, which may well have involved the issue of animal sacrifice. And in the context of the Book of Isaiah, a decision to challenge animal sacrifice in the Temple inevitably carried with it the implication of a Messianic vocation.

Emphasis on the issue of animal sacrifice in the Temple by Jesus would also explain why the movement which he led remained so small that Josephus did not even notice it. Important as this issue may have seemed to Jesus, it did not seem very important to most Jews at the time. Neither the Essenes nor the Pharisees, who were probably both somewhat critical of this practice, thought it of sufficient importance to make a major issue of it. The Sadducees of course favored animal sacrifice, while the Zealots did not object to it and may well have favored it too. Nor is there anything in the writings of the Qumran sect that implies opposition to animal sacrifice. Jesus and his tiny band of followers would have been relatively isolated in a militant opposition to this practice, and their isolation would in turn have made it easy for the authorities in charge of the Temple to dispose of Jesus without attracting much public attention. They could have had no stronger motive to see him condemned and executed than the fact that he was rejecting the very ritual on which the authority of the priests was largely based. That Jesus also declared himself "the Messiah" would probably have seemed a minor side issue to the Temple authorities compared with the damage which a determined attack on the practice of animal sacrifice could have inflicted on them. But in the eyes of the Ebionites, and even more in the eyes of Paul and the Christians, it was this side issue which was the important one, and the New Testament account of the trial and conviction of Jesus Christ by the Temple authorities was therefore composed with a view to highlighting his claim to be "the Messiah" and making that seem to be the cause of his execution.

Flusser, on page 589, shows that it was highly unlikely that Jesus was in fact condemned by a full session of the Sanhedrin as the New Testament asserts. He thinks the condemnation was probably the work of a "Temple committee" composed of the "chief priests". As for the Romans, they probably did not much care whether the Jews sacrificed animals or not, and therefore had no particular motive to either approve or disapprove of the condemnation of Jesus. Messianic agitation, on the other hand, was something which they consistently opposed, slaughtering literally thousands of Jews during that period for taking part in ceremonies led by would-be Messiahs. Had the claim of Jesus to be "the Messiah" been the major cause of his condemnation, the Romans would have required no prompting to execute him. Nor is there any other case on record in which the Temple authorities or the Sanhedrin condemned anyone for Messianic claims. Such claims were not uncommon, and there is little reason to believe that they were received with anything resembling the indignation which the New Testament ascribes to the Sanhedrin. If the claim of Jesus to be "the Messiah" was particularly insistent, this was most likely because he had to be "the Messiah" in order to authorize the abolition of animal sacrifice in the Temple. No lesser title, not even that of High Priest, would have been sufficient to authorize such a radical departure from tradition.

On the other hand, having adopted a Messianic self-concept, Jesus undoubtedly saw this as implying something more than the authority to abolish animal sacrifice. To his mind it probably implied the program of the Book of Isaiah as mediated through the doctrines of the Essenes and Pharisees. How he expected to implement this program is hard to say, since he had no realistic chance of doing so. His inability to attract more than a small following suggests that his contemporaries also thought his approach unrealistic. But once he was dead, his lack of realism became an advantage for his surviving followers. His idealism became an adornment for their small group, and this in turn attracted the attention of Paul. It was most likely Paul, and not the Ebionites, who hit upon the idea of portraying the death of Jesus as a "sacrifice" which could be viewed as a substitute for the animal sacrifice conducted in the Temple. As Schoeps puts it on page 62:

> Jewish Christianity clearly knows as little of a supernatural birth as of a soteriological interpretation of Jesus' death on the cross, such as the view which regarded Jesus as a vicarious atoning sacrifice. Since they rejected bloody sacrifices altogether as crass paganism, the Ebionite Jesus can neither have taught this nor by his death have put his seal on it - in contrast with the tradition of the primitive church preserved in I Corinthians 15:3. On the same basis they celebrated the Lord's Supper as a mere remembrance of table-fellowship with Jesus and replaced the cup of blood with a cup of water (according to Irenaeus and Epiphanius).

Indeed, the notion of Jesus as the "Lamb of God" who died so that others could live must have appeared barbaric and repulsive to the Ebionites. But for Paul it was an attractive notion, and in the wake of the destruction of the Temple in 70 CE, it became even more attractive for the emerging Christian church. In this way, what probably began as a movement to abolish animal sacrifice turned into a cult of what amounted to human sacrifice, whose emotional resonance was vastly enhanced by the large number of Jews who had in fact been murdered by the Romans, many by crucifixion.

The more the Christians harped on the theme of the "sacrifice" of Jesus, the more they had to regard him as a god. This process was already well advanced by the time the "gospels" were written, and this may explain why they do not present Jesus as a foe of animal sacrifice. Reforming the rites of the Temple was not a very big ambition for a god in human form whose alleged destiny was to reform the conduct of the entire human race and assure its heavenly future as well. Furthermore, the more the Christians emphasized the concept of the death of Jesus as a "sacrifice", the less eager would they have been to place too much emphasis on the theme of the abolition of sacrifice. And since the Temple was gone in any case, dropping the issue of animal sacrifice within it did not cost the Christians anything. To the contrary, it cleared the way for them to adopt the position that the destruction of the Temple was a punishment for the failure of the Jews to accept Jesus as their Messiah. This theme was incorporated into the "gospels" in the form of the "prediction" by Jesus that the Temple would be destroyed. And for many centuries thereafter, the Christians adopted a stance of implacable hatred for the very concept of the Temple, to the point where the Byzantine rulers of what they called "Palestine" used the site of the former Temple as a garbage dump.

Looking for the real Jesus in the New Testament is like looking for the Temple underneath a garbage dump. All we can learn from the New Testament is that the real Jesus was what might be called an Isaiahist. He took the Book of Isaiah seriously, too seriously for his own good. Others then used his excessive idealism as a basis for their own ambitions. It was those ambitions that shaped the version of the Messianic ideal which the Christians developed. In this version, Jewish Messianism began with Isaiah and was fulfilled by Jesus. Jesus was the perfect Messiah, whose every act and thought as portrayed in the New Testament fulfilled some Messianic prophecy. How foolish of the Jews not to know this! But of course the Jewish people did not need a perfect Messiah, just a successful one. The Christians knew this too, and therefore they had to find some way of depicting Jesus as successful in his own right. Their method is well known: they portrayed Jesus as a "miracle worker" who could raise people from the dead, walk on water and so forth. No doubt they received the inspiration for these legends from the Ebionites, but they went to some lengths to embellish them, adding such features as the "virgin birth" entirely on their own. The resulting story of the life and death of Jesus Christ is encapsulated in "miracles" from beginning to end. The only problem is, when the Christians hear stories of similar "miracles" in non-Christian cultures, they do not call them "miracles", but rather "magic".

Jesus the Magician

It was as a magician that Jesus was known in traditional Jewish rabbinic circles. This view was not derived from the New Testament, which the rabbis didn't read, but from a Hebrew tract called the "Toldot Yeshu", or "Story of Jesus". No one knows exactly when this tract was written, but it was in general circulation among Jewish rabbis and scholars from at least the 10th century onwards. It was a kind of parody of the New Testament in which the "virgin birth" was explained as the result of Mary having sex with a Roman soldier named Panthera, meaning "panther" in Hebrew, at the time she was menstruating. Her son was therefore known as "Yeshu ben Panthera". According to Joseph Klausner, on page 24 of *Jesus of Nazareth*, the reason this name was chosen is because "pandera" in Greek means "virgin". The "Toldot Yeshu" went on to recount how Yeshu ben Panthera performed various magical acts with the aid of the illegitimate use of the Holy Name but was eventually condemned by the rabbinical sages and hanged on a cabbage stem. The moral of the story was that Jesus had been justly condemned, not for trying to be "the Messiah", but for practicing magic.

Why didn't the rabbis adopt the obvious course of simply denying that the miracles described in the New Testament actually took place? It would seem that they couldn't because such an approach would have undermined the foundations of their own faith. There are also miracles in Jewish tradition, particularly in the story of Moses in the Book of Exodus. In order to defend their own miracles, the rabbis were therefore forced to stigmatize the Christian miracles as magic. In so doing, the rabbis paid involuntary tribute to the effectiveness of the Christian tactic of surrounding Jesus with miracles. This tactic had the effect of placing Jesus in the same class as Moses, who is the only historic figure in Tanach whose life is likewise surrounded with miracles. Moreover, it was consistent with the ideology of the Book of Isaiah, whose awaited Savior would have required a good deal of divine help to accomplish all that he was supposed to accomplish. It is very likely that Jesus expected just such help, which was, unfortunately for him, not forthcoming. But that is just the point: miracles don't happen. Jewish tradition did not really require a miracle worker as Messiah, simply a successful leader. By insisting on the performance of miracles as the proof of Messianic status, the Christians were in effect inventing a new version of the Messianic ideal, one which placed more emphasis on the Messiah's supernatural qualities than on any other point.

Supernaturalism had always been a part of the Messianic message, but the Christian notion of a divine Messiah who proved his divine status by working miracles on earth was nonetheless something new. In Jewish tradition, supernaturalism had been incorporated into the Messianic message in two fairly well defined ways. On the one hand, it attached itself as a kind of penumbra to the notion of a mortal Messiah who would restore the Jewish nation and way of life; and on the other hand, it appeared full blown in the notion of a divine Messiah who would rule over the entire world during the "last days". In neither case was supernatural power viewed as "proof" of Messianic status. The mortal Messiah was expected to prove his status by succeeding, while the divine Messiah did not have to prove anything because his advent was supposed to be accompanied by God's direct intervention in history in the form of the resurrection of the dead, the Last Judgment and so forth. From a Jewish point of view, the notion of a divine Messiah who appeared on earth, worked a series of magic tricks and then disappeared again was absurd, and the story of Yeshu ben Panthera in the "Toldot Yeshu" faithfully reflected this sense of the absurdity of the Christian message. But from a Greco-Roman point of view, the Christian version of the Messianic ideal evidently made a good deal of sense, and it is important to understand why.

In the first place, it made sense because it tied in with an already well established tradition in Greco-Roman society of the veneration of a divine figure who was supposed to bring peace and harmony to the world but was murdered instead. W.K.C. Guthrie in *Orpheus and Greek Religion* provides a detailed exposition of just how this tradition arose. It was the creation of the Orphics, an organized religious movement which originated in Greece in the 6th century BCE. According to Orphic theology, Dionysos was born of the rape of Persephone by Zeus. Zeus intended him to institute a new age of

111

peace and harmony, but instead he was killed and eaten as a baby by the evil Titans. This story provided the mythical basis for a ritual in which the Orphics consumed bread and wine as symbols of the flesh and blood of the martyred baby Dionysos, claiming thereby to assure themselves of eternal life. In later centuries, these ideas and the ritual associated with them were disseminated on a wide scale throughout the Greco-Roman world in many different forms. On page 265, Guthrie reproduces a seal-cylinder or amulet dating from the 3rd or 4th century CE showing a crucified figure with the inscription, "Orpheus Bakkikos". Orpheus was considered the prophet of the advent of Dionysos in Orphic theology, and Guthrie explains the amulet as follows: "This has usually been supposed to be the work of some Gnostic sect exhibiting a syncretism of Orphic and Christian ideas." Such "syncretism" was only natural, since as Guthrie notes on page 267: "Both Christ and Dionysos were the sons of God, and both suffered, died and were resurrected."

In the second place, it made sense because those Jews, like Paul and his followers, who were striving to assimilate to Greco-Roman society, could not have had much faith in the possibility of a Jewish victory over Rome even before the destruction of the Temple in 70 CE. From their point of view, the whole idea of a victorious Messiah who was a mere mortal was therefore problematic. The only Messiah who could have made sense to them was a divine Messiah, and it was only natural for them to want a glimpse of him even before the "last days". Brandon summarizes Paul's attitude towards Jesus on page 11 of *Jesus and the Zealots* as follows:

> He clearly regarded the historical Jesus, the Christ *kata sarka* in his terminology, as the temporary incarnation of a pre-existent divine being, whom he variously calls 'the Lord of glory', 'the Lord' and 'the Son of God'.

These ideas were rejected by the Ebionites, along with the cannibal ritual associated with them, but the more distant in time and space from the "historical Jesus" that the cult of Jesus became, the more plausible they seemed. There were, after all, numerous descriptions of a divine Messiah in Jewish "eschatological" literature, and the Christians did their best to preserve these texts as "proof" that the concept of a supernatural Jesus was consistent with Jewish tradition. Above all, the destruction of the Temple and devastation of the land of Israel by the Romans made it appear to the surviving Jews in the Diaspora that a divine Messiah was the only Messiah they would ever know. Conversion to Christianity in this context could easily appear as a way of preserving the Messianic ideal in the midst of its massive defeat.

In the third place, it made sense because it fit in with a general trend towards increased belief in magic and the supernatural in Greco-Roman society. Many historians have commented on this trend, which was mainly a result of the establishment of the Roman empire and the gradual loss of national independence and political rights by its constituent parts. Rationalist philosophies like Stoicism or Epicureanism declined during this period, to be superseded by Gnostic cults and a mystical neo-Platonism. The Gnostics and neo-Platonists taught that the material world was only an illusion or a passing phase and that true reality was spiritual in nature. The spread of these ideas on the philosophic plane was accompanied by a proliferation of "mystery religions" and a growing interest in astrology and magical practices. The cult of Jesus the Magician was at first just one of many such cults. As Christian historians never tire of repeating, it nonetheless outdistanced its rivals because of its superior ethical and moral stature. Christian ethics and morality, however, were almost entirely derived from Jewish teachings, particularly those of the Essenes and Pharisees. But in a world where Jews were being murdered in the millions and conversion to Judaism was, from 135 CE onwards, a crime punishable by death, non-Jews who were attracted to Jewish ethics and morality had no real alternative to Christianity. Christianity was thus placed in the enviable position of having its Judaism and eating it too. It preserved and disseminated a large part of Jewish tradition in the form of the "Old Testament", the "Apocrypha and Pseudepigrapha" and the sayings of Jesus, while at the same time vilifying the Jews and practicing a magical rite which promised eternal life to all those would pretend to eat the flesh and drink the blood of a dead Jew.

Christian anti-Semitism was rooted first and foremost in the resentment which the Ebionites must have felt as a result of the condemnation and execution of Jesus. This resentment was undoubtedly heightened by their later conflicts with the Jewish authorities and found expression in their flight from Jerusalem at the time of the rebellion against the Romans and subsequent move to Jordan. But conflicts between contending Jewish factions were common at that time and nevertheless did not result in the formation of anti-Semitic religions. The decisive step in the development of a Christian anti-Semitic tradition was the founding of the Christian religion by Saint Paul. As Flusser notes in *Judaism and the Origins of Christianity,* the teachings of Paul were much closer in spirit to those of the Qumran sect than the teachings of Jesus. In particular, Paul was much given to what Flusser calls "Dualism", the division of the human race into good guys and bad guys, and in Paul's scheme of thing the Jews were numbered among the bad guys. He could hardly have thought otherwise, considering that he was denying the possibility of their liberation from the Romans and exhorting them to eat another Jew in effigy instead. Paul's view of the Jews as a diabolic element came to pervade the entire New Testament. It appears not only in his letters and in the "gospels" but especially in The Acts of the Apostles. Klausner, on page 229 of *From Jesus To Paul*, characterizes The Acts of the Apostles as follows:

> For the whole book is saturated with one "ruling idea", the beginning of which is already to be found even in the Gospel according to Mark, although it does not come to extreme expression until in Acts. This idea is that the Jews are *the source of evil*. They persecute the Christians and slander them before the Roman authorities; and these authorities are charitably inclined toward the Christians and do not inhibit Christianity except under pressure from the Jews.

Following the destruction of the Temple and the Roman mass murders, this attitude on the part of Paul and his associates came to serve the emerging Christian church in good stead. It made it possible for the Christians to disassociate themselves from the Jews - which might otherwise have been hard to do considering the prominence of Jewish texts in Christian theology - and thereby assure at least the possibility of the toleration of Christianity by the Romans.

In fact, the Christian church in the 2nd century CE was confronted with a strong push on the part of a faction of Gnostic Chris-

114

tians, led by Marcion, to completely sever its ties with Judaism, which the Marcionites identified with the diabolic forces said to control the material world. But the Marcionites were eventually defeated and branded as "heretics", essentially because Christianity could not sever its ties with Judaism without also abandoning its claim that Jesus was "the Messiah". This claim was an essential part of Christian ideology, the foundation on which the identification of Jesus as the "Son of God" was erected, and hence the ultimate basis for the ritual of eating Jesus which the Gnostics themselves found so appealing. In order to "prove" that Jesus was "the Messiah", the Christians had to use Jewish texts, and their use of these texts also had the effect of making Christianity more attractive to former Jews or Jewish sympathizers. In this way the Christian religion developed a profoundly mixed message, pro-Jewish and anti-Jewish at one and the same time, which has given rise to both pro-Jewish and anti-Jewish movements and tendencies throughout its history. As a rule, however, the more prominent the image of Jesus the Magician in any given Christian sect or denomination, the more anti-Semitic it is likely to be. The Gnostic Christians, who were violently anti-Semitic, were so taken with the idea of Jesus the Magician that they composed a whole collection of tracts that never made it into the New Testament attributing all kinds of additional supernatural acts and powers to the great Jesus.

The cult of Jesus the Magician is really the flip side of the cult of Jesus the Victim. The greater the magician Christians imagine Jesus to be, the more indignant they become at the refusal of the Jews to worship him and the Jewish role in the events leading up to his death. They do not notice that Jewish history is filled with martyrs, yet Jewish tradition places very little emphasis on the circumstances surrounding their martyrdom. What is remembered is how they lived, what they accomplished, what they stood for. Rabbi Akiva was tortured to death by the Romans in 135 CE by having the skin peeled off his body, but there are no pictures of a flayed rabbi Akiva in Jewish synagogues. It is the life and teachings of rabbi Akiva that are remembered, and the fact that he hailed Simon bar Kochba as "the Messiah". This fact must have impressed the Christians too, for it was from this time onwards that the radical faction among them began to place increasing emphasis on the concept of "the Second Coming".

This concept ended up serving as a vehicle for the reintroduction of a more Jewish version of the Messianic ideal into Christian thought. The Christ of "the Second Coming" was of course no longer a victim but rather a triumphant figure called upon to judge and rule over the world. He did not have to be a magician because his role was to succeed. For the worshippers of Jesus the Magician, on the other hand, the main function of Jesus was to provide them with a sacramental basis for eternal life. This approach could and did coexist with all kinds of tyrannical regimes, since the material world was, according to this view, merely a waiting room for eternity.

The history of Christianity during the first 300 years or so of its existence was one of constant tension and antagonism between the pro-Jewish and anti-Jewish elements in Christian thought. This tension was resolved early in the 4th century CE by the conversion of the Roman Caesar Constantine to Christianity. Constantine of course sided with the anti-Jewish faction, as reflected in the decision of the Council of Nicaea in 325 CE to adopt, under Constantine's prodding, the slogan "the Father and the Son" as the hallmark of the Christian faith. This slogan fairly reeked of Gnosticism and was based mainly on its constant use by the author of the "Gospel of John", whom modern scholars have had no difficulty identifying as a Gnostic Christian. The Gnostics had worshipped "the Father and the Son", meaning Zeus and Dionysos, long before they ever encountered Christianity. And for the Gnostics, there was no doubt that this slogan implied the biological parentage of "God the Father", seeing as Zeus had raped Perspehone to produce Dionysos in the original Orphic myth. Insistence on the biological parentage of "God the Father" also became the hallmark of both Greek Orthodox and Roman Catholic Christianity, giving rise to a whole series of Middle Eastern "heresies" which sought in one way or another to avoid the obvious inference that Christianity was based on the rape of Mary by God. Viewed in this light, the description of the parentage of Yeshu ben Panthera in the "Toldot Yeshu" must be seen as remarkably consistent with the "Orthodox" and "Catholic" conception of how Christianity got started.

The establishment of Christianity as the "Orthodox" or "Catholic" religion of the Roman empire assured the domination of the anti-Jewish faction within it for more than 1000 years. It was not until the

116

time of the Protestant Reformation in the 16th century that the pro-Jewish tendency in Christianity was able to reassert itself as something more than a marginal radical fringe of the established Christian churches. Yet from a Jewish point of view, even Protestant Christianity, which is far less anti-Semitic than either Greek Orthodox or Roman Catholic Christianity, brings to mind the well known Jewish saying: "With friends like these, who needs enemies?" There is simply no getting around the fact that "the Jews" are the villains of the New Testament. Well meaning Christians, of whom there have been many over the years, may choose to overlook this fact or strive to compensate for it in some way, but the fact remains. Perhaps at one time study of the New Testament was the only way for large numbers of people to familiarize themselves with the ethical and moral teachings of the Essenes and Pharisees as filtered through the sayings of Jesus. But due to the expansion of book publishing and other modern forms of communication, this is no longer true. Those who continue to insist on the sanctity of the New Testament testify thereby either to their indifference to or affirmation of its anti-Semitic content. They will not get to heaven no matter what they do, so they might as well stop eating Jesus.

Simon bar Kochba

Of all the Jewish leaders of the era of the "Jewish Wars", Simon bar Kochba was undoubtedly the one who came closest to being recognized by other Jews as "the Messiah". This was due in part to the fact that he was acclaimed as "King Messiah" by rabbi Akiva, and in part to the fact that he was the undisputed leader of a unified rebel movement that established a Jewish state in the land of Israel. This state issued coins and assumed all the trappings of sovereignty insofar as it was able to do so in the territory which it controlled. In short, Simon bar Kochba did what "the Messiah" was supposed to do, if only for a few years, and rabbi Akiva's recognition of him as "King Messiah" was undoubtedly based on this fact.

Little is reliably known about either bar Kochba or the revolt which he led due to the absence of any extensive historical account such as Josephus wrote about the first "Jewish War". The few direct references to him in rabbinical literature depict him as powerful but arrogant. It is said that he compelled his followers to cut off one of their fingers as a sign of devotion. It is said that he told his followers not to ask God for victory but merely for neutrality. It is said that he killed a rabbi who disagreed with him. No one knows whether these stories are true or legendary, but it seems likely that they have at least some basis in fact. The main thing which the Romans remembered about him is that their troops suffered such heavy losses in the fighting against the Jewish rebels whom he led that Hadrian decided not to celebrate a formal "triumph" when his army returned in victory to Rome at the end of the second "Jewish War". Simon bar Kochba himself is thought to have been killed when the Romans overran his last stronghold, Betar, in 135 CE.

The death of Simon bar Kochba brought to an end a period of approximately 200 years in duration during which numerous Jewish leaders in the land of Israel sought to revive the independent Jewish state which had been overthrown by Roman troops under the command of Pompey in 63 BCE. With increasing frequency, these leaders were hailed by their followers as "the Messiah", until the last of them achieved general recognition of this status. It was this sequence of events which elevated the concept of "the Messiah" to the position of a powerful symbol of inspired leadership throughout the Middle East and the Mediterranean region. Christianity fed on this history and rose to prominence because it offered a version of the Messianic ideal that was able to survive the circumstances of its defeat. However, it did so only by falsifying the true nature of this ideal and transforming it into a cult of magic tricks. Even the concept of an "eschatological" Messiah, which was rooted in Jewish tradition as well as the Christian doctrine of "the Second Coming", was at bottom only a secondary reflection and elaboration of the actual struggle of the Jewish people for national liberation. This struggle was conducted by millions of people, most of whom were killed in the process, and it is to their heroism and spirit of self-sacrifice that the subsequent prominence of the Messianic ideal is largely due.

In terms of Jewish tradition, the effect of the events of the period 63 BCE to 135 CE on the evolution of the Messianic ideal was twofold. In the first place, it resulted in the adoption of the expression, "the Messiah", as the only conceivable term for an awaited leader who would bring about the restoration of Jewish sovereignty and independence. All the other words and expressions which had flourished during the period prior to 135 CE as names for such a leader now disappeared from general use. And in the second place, it confronted the surviving leaders of the Jewish people, who were mainly rabbis, with the difficult task of developing a version of the Messianic ideal which could survive the circumstances of its defeat yet still distinguish itself from the Christian version. The resulting Jewish concept of "the Messiah" has remained little known and little understood outside of Jewish circles, and yet it has exercised a considerable influence on world history all the same. For want of a better word, let's call it the Unknown Messiah.

Chapter Five:
The Unknown Messiah

Writing at the end of the 15th century, the Spanish Jewish leader Don Isaac Abravanel felt the need to prove to Jewish and Christian readers alike why Jesus Christ could not have been "the Messiah". He therefore developed a comprehensive list of all the events and circumstances which were supposed to be associated with the advent of "the Messiah" in Jewish tradition. His point was that most of these events and circumstances did not occur during the life of Jesus Christ, and therefore Jesus Christ could not have been "the Messiah". On page 207 of his admirable biography, *Don Isaac Abravanel*, Benzion Netanyahu summarizes Abravanel's list as follows:

> Upon surveying all biblical passages which could have reference to redemption, Abravanel found, among its unquestionable characteristics, that redemption could come only after a long exile; that the Ten Tribes exiled to Assyria would return; that God's terrible vengeance would be wrought upon the nations who persecuted Israel; that those among the nations who survived the punishment would accept the true faith; that the dead would be resurrected; that the future redemption would resemble in many ways the Egyptian exodus; that Providence would return to Israel to an extent even greater than was manifest on Mt. Sinai; that there would be a wide recurrence of prophecy, miracles and divine signs; and finally, that a King of the House of David, imbued with the spirit of God, would rule over Israel, and his word be law even to the remotest islands of the world. These are some of the basic conditions which must be present at the time of redemption.

Netanyahu adds on page 226: "The three most significant features which will mark the epoch of the messianic arrival are, in Abravanel's own words, "Revenge upon our enemies, the Redemption of Israel, and the Resurrection of the dead"."

Abravanel thought all this would probably happen in the year 1503 CE, but as it turned out he was mistaken.

What is most striking about Abravanel's image of the Messianic era is his indiscriminate mixture of natural and supernatural events without any attempt to distinguish between the two. Was Abravanel expecting a divine or a human Messiah? It is hard to say. In the "Apocrypha and Pseudepigrapha", it is usually quite clear which of the two is intended, but by Abravanel's time this distinction had broken down. A new conception of "the Messiah" had taken hold, one for which the distinction between natural and supernatural was essentially irrelevant. This conception had its roots in the period following the defeat and death of Simon bar Kochba, the period of the emergence of rabbinical Judaism as the only "orthodox" form of Jewish thought and belief. Indifference to the distinction between natural and supernatural was one of the hallmarks of rabbinical thought, as it was of medieval thought in general. Abravanel was a kind of transitional figure, one who derived most of his intellectual categories from medieval sources but who was in spirit and temperament much closer to the Renaissance and the modern age. Forgotten today, he had a major influence on his contemporaries, stimulating a revived interest in Jewish Messianism among Jews and Christians alike. Netanyahu, on page 251, sees him as "launching the most potent messianic movement in Jewish history" as well as exercising "a profound and lasting influence on the Christian world as well", and concludes: "Indeeed, between the ages of the Reformation and the Enlightenment, no Jewish writer enjoyed greater fame or aroused such widespread interest and discussion, as did Abravanel."

Between the time of Simon bar Kochba and that of Don Isaac Abravanel, Jewish Messianism was of little interest to anyone except the Jews themselves. Rabbinical views on the subject of "the Messiah" were scattered in Hebrew or Aramaic texts which hardly anyone but Jews could read and which no one felt compelled to translate into other languages.

Jewish Messianic movements, which were surprisingly numerous, nonetheless attracted little attention because they were invariably local, confined to a single city or region, and had little or no impact on events in the land of Israel itself. Yet within Jewish society, the Messianic ideal remained very much alive. Indeed, it eventually became an integral part of rabbinic thought whose "orthodox" status was even more firmly established than it had been in the days of the uprisings against Rome. Legends and beliefs about "the Messiah" were also widespread in Jewish popular culture. Maimonides, writing in the 12th century, declared belief in the coming of "the Messiah" to be one of the thirteen "Articles of Faith" of the Jewish religion, in which all Jews were required to believe. This belief was formulated as follows: "I believe with perfect faith in the coming of the Messiah, and though he tarry, I will wait daily for his coming."

Who was the Messiah for whom "orthodox" Jews were required to wait? Was there also an "orthodox" conception of precisely who he was supposed to be, what he was supposed to be like? This does not appear to have been the case. Maimonides had certain ideas on this subject, others had different ideas. What came to be called "Orthodox Judaism" deliberately avoided any attempt to compile an official list of the presumed characteristics of "the Messiah". The previous list, in the Book of Isaiah, had worked out badly. The one thing everyone knew is that his advent would coincide with the return of the Jewish people to the land of Israel and the reestablishment of a Jewish kingdom there. Beyond that he remained something of a mystery, except to the readers of the Talmud. Even though they are nowhere assembled in one place, there are numerous remarks about "the Messiah" in the Talmud and related rabbinical literature. Taken together they constitute a view of the Messianic ideal which was specific to rabbinical circles and reflected rabbinical culture in particular as well as Jewish national culture in general. For the rabbis, the Unknown Messiah was the Messiah who was born on Tisha B'Av.

Tisha B'Av

Tisha B'Av, the Ninth of Av, was the date on the Jewish calendar on which both the first and second Temples had been destroyed. It was treated as a fast day and a day of mourning in rabbinical culture. Although rabbinical Judaism was not centered around the Temple, which no longer existed, and although the prophetic tradition out of which rabbinical Judaism emerged was critical of the sacrificial rites of the Temple, the destruction of the Temple was nonetheless treated by the rabbis as a major catastrophe. This was the context in which the belief gradually took hold that the Messiah, who was seen as a heavenly figure who already existed, had been born on Tisha B'Av.

Jacob Neusner, on page 94 of *Messiah In Context*, notes that the Yerushalmi - the version of the Talmud that was compiled in the land of Israel - seeks to substantiate the claim that "the Messiah was born on the day the Temple was destroyed". The Yerushalmi was completed around 400 CE and incorporated material dating from the 3rd and 4th centuries CE. Neusner, who has written extensively on the subject of the origins of rabbinic Judaism, believes that it was during this period that the concept of "the Messiah" began to assume a prominent position in rabbinical thought. In the Mishnah, a key rabbinical text compiled around 200 CE, there were a few brief references to "the days of the Messiah" or "the footprints of the Messiah", but no great importance was attached to this theme. As Neusner puts it on page 30:

> For the philosophers of the Mishnah the Messiah figure presents no rich resource of myth or symbol. The Messiah forms part of the inherited, but essentially undifferentiated, background of factual materials. The figure is neither to be neglected nor to be exploited.

But in the Yerushalmi, notes Neusner on page 93, "we find a clear effort to identify the person of the Messiah and to confront the claim that a specific, named individual had been, or would be, the Messiah." That individual was Simon bar Kochba, whose Messianic status was denied by the Yerushalmi.

In another of his books, *The Four Stages Of Rabbinic Judaism*, Neusner further developed this same contrast between the treatment of the theme of "the Messiah" in the Mishnah and in the Yerushalmi, the Talmud of the Land of Israel. Neusner states on page 195:

> In the Talmud of the Land of Israel by contrast we find a fully exposed doctrine of not only a Messiah, but *the* Messiah: who he is, how we will know him, what we must do to bring him.

According to the authors of the Yerushalmi, the Messiah would be a Torah scholar like themselves and would come when the Jewish people fully accepted the laws of God. This view was expressed in such statements as, "If Israel repents for one day, forthwith the son of David will come", and "If Israel would keep a single Sabbath in the proper way, forthwith the son of David will come." In the meanwhile the Messiah was thought to reside in heaven, and in time quite an elaborate picture was developed in rabbinical literature as to precisely what he was doing there.

Why was the Messianic ideal integrated into rabbinic thought during the 3rd and 4th centuries CE? It is often forgotten that the immediate cause of the revolt led by Simon bar Kochba was the decision of the Roman Caesar Hadrian to outlaw circumcision and other Jewish religious practices in 132 CE. It was in large part for this reason that the majority of rabbis, led by Akiva, supported the revolt. The ban on circumcision actually remained a permanent feature of Roman law, but it was amended by Hadrian's successor, Antoninus Pius, to permit circumcision of sons of Jewish parents. The Romans thus abandoned Hadrian's program of eliminating Judaism altogether, while at the same time effectively preventing the further spread of Judaism within the Roman empire. The surviving rabbis in the land of Israel, whose Jewish population still numbered some 750,000 in the wake of the revolt, were permitted by the Romans to act as judges in civil cases which could be adjudicated under Jewish law. With Roman approval, the rabbinical courts thus became the sole remnant of Jewish legal and political authority, and this situation, taken together with the memory of the failure of the two massive revolts against Rome, inclined the rabbis to shun anything which smacked of Messianic agitation. They did not actually repudiate the Messianic ideal, in the name of which so many had died, but they kept it at arm's length, focusing instead on the details of Jewish law.

Rabbinic authority in the land of Israel under Roman rule reached its height around 200 CE, the time of the compilation of the Mishnah. The head of the rabbinic Sanhedrin at that time, Judah "the Prince", enjoyed great personal prestige and was treated by the Romans with some of the deference usually accorded to heads of state. But the 3rd century CE was a period of civil war and economic decline throughout the Roman empire, and this trend was reflected in increasing unrest in the land of Israel. Michael Avi-Yonah in *The Jews of Palestine* sees the 3rd century as a period of declining rabbinic authority and growing Messianic agitation conducted by popular preachers and even a few rabbis. On page 131 he describes the following prophecy from this time: "According to Rabbi Levi the Messiah from the House of Joseph will, after rebuilding the Temple, march upon Rome and conquer it as Joshua conquered Jericho." Then, early in the 4th century CE, the Roman Caesar Constantine converted to Christianity. As Avi-Yonah notes on page 165, Constantine was personally hostile to Judaism and his letters are filled with such phrases as "the lawless Jews", "the perjured Jews" and "the impure ones". He initiated a program, which was continued by his successors, of building Christian churches in the land of Israel and trying to stimulate Christian settlement there. This was followed in 339 CE by a series of decrees by Constantius 2 banning intermarriage and other contacts between Christians and Jews. This was the first comprehensive anti-Jewish legislation in the Roman empire since the days of Hadrian and inaugurated a period of growing anti-Jewish activity on the part of the Christian Caesars and Christian church which continued right down to the time of the rise of Islam in the 7th century CE.

These were the circumstances which led to the integration of the Messianic ideal into rabbinic thought as reflected in the Yerushalmi. But the version of the Messianic ideal which was developed by the rabbis differed significantly from the traditional one. As Neusner notes on page 201 of yet another of his books, *Judaism in Society*, the Yerushalmi "treats the messianic hope as something gradual, to be worked toward, not a sudden cataclysmic event." The way to bring the Messiah was to observe Jewish law, and of course the ultimate authorities on the observance of Jewish law were the rabbis themselves. However, there remained a huge gap in rabbinic thought between the gradual, mundane process which was supposed to bring the Messiah and the advent of the Messiah himself. As Greenstone puts it on page 107 of *The Messiah Idea In Jewish History*, with reference to the Talmudic period: "Unconsciously, and perhaps against the wish of the teachers, the person of the Messiah was surrounded with a halo of Divine and supernatural qualities, and the age of his coming was associated with marvellous deeds and supermundane beings." The gap between Messianic process and Messianic result in rabbinic thought reflected the unpleasant fact that observance of Jewish law, no matter how perfect, could not actually bring into being a Jewish army capable of gaining control of the land of Israel and establishing a Jewish state. Unwilling to give up the Messianic ideal yet unable to really implement it, the rabbis therefore adopted the doctrine of a natural process giving rise to a supernatural result.

The Unknown Messiah was the Messiah of a defeated people. He was born on the very day of their defeat to show that the root of the future victory would be found in the ruins of the past defeat. That root, the rabbis believed, was fidelity to Jewish law. From a rabbincal standpoint, the only possible reason why an all-powerful God would permit the Jewish people to be defeated is because the Jewish people had sinned. This view, which was rooted in the teachings of the prophets, made it necessary for the rabbis to adopt a stance of continually scolding the Jewish people and holding up its alleged faults for all to see. Christianity was in many ways but an extension and amplification of this way of looking at the Jewish people, a way that was fundamentally unjust from the start. I am sure that a statistical study, if it could be undertaken, would show that the Jews of ancient times sinned less, not more, than their neighbors. But the rabbis harped on the sins of the Jews because that was the one way they could envisage eventually winning. If the Temple was destroyed because of the sins of the Jews, then the Temple could be restored by conforming to God's intent. Implicit in this doctrine was the somewhat novel idea that the Jewish people could induce God to send the Messiah. The traditional view was that the Messiah would come in conformance with God's inscrutable will and not a moment sooner or later. The Talmudic sages did not directly challenge this view, but they essentially abandoned it in favor of a different view, one which placed the Jewish people at the center of a cosmic struggle that would end in victory and the restoration of the Jewish nation in the land of Israel.

In this way the concept of "the Messiah" became a kind of mediating term linking the natural and supernatural aspects of the process which was to bring about the ultimate victory of the Jewish people. Joseph Dan in *The Ancient Jewish Mysticism* shows that "the Messiah" was not the only mediating term of this kind. During the Talmudic period, there also flourished a genre of Jewish religious literature known as "literature of the chariot". Certain rabbis, and Akiva in particular, were pictured as riding an imaginary chariot to heaven, where they were said to encounter various gigantic supernatural beings in God's heavenly court. These beings were described as allies of the Jewish people whom God would unleash upon the world when the time was right. That time would come when the Jewish people was deserving of it, and this in turn depended upon the efforts of the rabbis to convince the Jewish people to observe God's laws. Needless to say, rabbinical thought defined the rabbis themselves as the key to Jewish success. This view was set forth in one such "mystical" work, "Prince of the Torah", where the rabbinical leadership is addressed by God, on page 152 of Dan's book, as follows:

> You will be known as those who aid the community, you will

127

be referred to as those who help mankind; the determination of the months will come from you and the proclamation of the leap years from your storehouse of wisdom. Through you leaders will be anointed and by your mouths the heads of the courts proclaimed. You will establish the exilarchs, the judges of the cities with your authority, for the welfare of the world will come from you, and there will be none who will dispute it.

This was an idealized description of the role which the rabbis actually sought to play during the Talmudic period, a role which defined them as the saviors not only of the Jewish community but the entire world.

In time the various supernatural beings situated in heaven in the "literature of the chariot" tended to coalesce into one such being, "the Messiah" himself. And this composite Messiah was pictured as a kind of collective entity whose soul was linked to the souls of the entire Jewish people. He lived in heaven but felt the sufferings of the Jewish people on earth and eagerly awaited the day when he would be allowed to lead them to victory. Eventually correct observance of Jewish law came to be seen as a way, not merely of bringing the Messiah, but of actually elevating him to his full stature. This view persisted right down to modern times and was especially pronounced in the writings of the early Hasidim of the 18th century. Gershom Scholem on page 199 of *The Messianic Idea in Judaism* cites Nachum of Chernobyl as follows:

> Everybody in Israel has to restore and to prepare that part of the structure of the Messiah which belongs to his own soul...for the Messiah will be a complete structure composed of all the souls of Israel which are six hundred thousand as they were contained within Adam before the fall. Therefore everyone in Israel should prepare that part corresponding to his part in the soul of the Messiah which belongs to his own soul until the whole structure will be restored and established and then there will be a permanent and universal *yihud*, realization of unity.

And Ben Zion Bokser, on page 243 of *The Jewish Mystical Tradition*, cites a similar statement by Nachman of Bratslav:

> Each person will bring to fruition his own messianic element, ascending from level to level, in slow stages, until God's kingship will become fully manifest; and this state corresponds to what we mean by the coming of the messiah.

In this view, every action of every Jewish individual was also an action in a cosmic drama whereby the Jewish people, under the proper leadership, would gradually elevate the Messiah in heaven to the point where he would be able to carry out his mission on earth.

To call this version of the Messianic ideal unrealistic would be to understate the case. To be sure, there were a few rabbinical thinkers who took a different approach. The most important was Maimonides, who said that the Messiah would establish a Jewish kingdom in the land of Israel but otherwise life would continue as before, only more prosperous and spiritual. The resurrection of the dead and other wonders would only come later and would not be a feature of the Messianic age. Greenstone on page 146 of *The Messiah Idea In Jewish History* calls the writings of Maimonides on this subject "the first rational picture of the Messianic age that had appeared for many centuries". But as shown by the characteristics of the Messianic age described by Abravanel at the end of the 15th century, the teachings of Maimonides on this point were not widely accepted. The dominant view in rabbinical circles right down to modern times was that of the Messiah as a supernatural being and his advent as a supernatural event, which could however be hastened and even caused by the correct performance of religious ritual. Moreover, starting with the "literature of the chariot" and continuing with Kabbalah, there gradually emerged in Jewish tradition what amounted to an image of the supernatural Messiah, one which emphasized his gigantic stature, compassionate nature and heavenly activities.

Just what was the value of the rabbinical version of the Messianic ideal in terms of actually bringing about the restoration of Jewish rule in the land of Israel? It could be argued that it kept hope alive, but the hope which it preserved was a forlorn one. In real life, no amount of correct observance of religious ritual could bring into being a Jewish army capable of accomplishing the task of the Messiah. Didn't the rabbis know this? It's hard to say. What is clear is that in the process of developing an image of the Unknown Messiah, rabbinical thought also developed certain clues which pointed beyond this image to a more practical and realistic conception of the Messianic ideal. In particular, rabbinical thought consistently associated this image with two rabbis who had been contemporaries of one another, Akiva and Shimon bar Yochai. Akiva is the main actual historical figure in the "literature of the chariot", while Shimon bar Yochai was the main actual historical figure in the literature of Kabbalah. Akiva also figures prominently in a number of anecdotes in the Talmud concerning Messianic speculation. And Akiva and Shimon bar Yochai are the central figures in rabbinical tradition in connection with the little known Jewish holiday of Lag Ba'Omer. An examination of the history of this holiday will provide a convenient way of bringing out a shadowy figure who stands concealed behind the already concealed figure of the Unknown Messiah.

Lag Ba'Omer

Lag Ba'Omer means "Thirty Three In The Sheaf", a reference to the sheaf of wheat which is associated with the period between Pesach and Shvuot in Jewish tradition. This period is supposed to consist of seven times seven weeks, or 49 days in all, and Lag Ba'Omer is the 33rd day in this sequence. It is the one day during the period of the Omer when weddings and other joyous festivities are permitted to be celebrated. The period of the Omer was traditionally viewed as a time of tension and anxiety, originally because of concern about the growth of the spring crop. Shvuot, the "Festival of Weeks", was also known as the "Festival of First Fruits", and the harvest of the first fruits of the spring crop at this time was seen as symbolically bringing the Omer period of anxiety to an end. However, there is no mention of Lag

Ba'Omer in Tanach, and it does not appear that this holiday was celebrated in ancient times. It is first mentioned in the Talmud, in connection with certain stories about rabbi Akiva.

The gist of these stories is that rabbi Akiva's pupils were struck by a plague during the period of the Omer, and for this reason this period was to be observed as a time of mourning, during which festivities could not be held. Yehuda Liebes discusses this custom in his illuminating book, *Studies in the Zohar*. He refers to Lag BaOmer in this context, noting on page 40 that "tradition holds it to be the day on which death ceased striking down R. Akiba's pupils, and so also that on which his new disciples were ordained." He adds:

> The tradition about *Lag Ba-'Omer* is cited, moreover, as a source for the ruling that the mourning customs practiced during the *Omer* period in memory of the deaths of R. Akiva's disciples be stopped on that day.

Liebes and others believe that the references to a "plague" killing rabbi Akiva's students were actually cryptic allusions to the massacres carried out by the Romans during the "second Jewish War". This war was initiated by Hadrian's ban on Judaism, and the Romans therefore made a point of attacking Torah students during it, killing some by wrapping them in their Torah scrolls and setting them on fire. The period of the Omer, which was already defined as a period of anxiety in Jewish tradition, was then adopted by the authors of the Talmud as an appropriate time to mourn the victims of the Roman onslaught. However they made an exception for Lag BaOmer, suggesting that they viewed it as a day on which the Roman attack was somehow temporarily halted.

In later centuries, Lag BaOmer also came to be associated with rabbi Shimon bar Yochai, a contemporary of Akiva. Liebes discusses this association, which he attributes to an early Kabbalistic belief that the "Idra Rabba", or session of the Sanhedrin supposedly convoked by Shimon bar Yochai, was held on Lag BaOmer. However, in later centuries a tradition developed among Kabbalists that Shimon bar Yochai had died on Lag BaOmer. Starting perhaps in the 16th cen-

131

tury, Kabbalists living in the land of Israel began to congregate on Lag BaOmer at the tomb of Shimon bar Yochai in the village of Meron in Galilee. A practice developed of lighting huge bonfires on this occasion and treating it as an opportunity to proclaim the virtues of Shimon bar Yochai. This practice has continued to this day, and each year tens of thousands of Hasidim gather at Meron on Lag BaOmer to commemorate what they view as the anniversary of the death of Shimon bar Yochai. They do not, however, treat this day as an occasion for mourning, but rather celebrate it and continue the tradition which started in Talmudic times of holding weddings on Lag BaOmer.

Shimon bar Yochai was an actual historical figure who joined with Akiva in supporting the revolt led by Simon bar Kochba. After the defeat of the revolt, Shimon bar Yochai supposedly hid from the Romans for 13 years in a cave near Meron until it was safe to come out. He was not an especially prominent figure in his own lifetime, but he was remembered in rabbinical tradition because he had escaped from the Romans. A 13th century Spanish Kabbalist named Moses de Leon then made him the hero of the "Zohar", a lengthy fictitious account of conversations between Shimon bar Yochai and his disciples concerning the esoteric meaning of the Torah. The "Zohar" was accepted as genuine in rabbinical circles because it was written in Aramaic, and it came to be considered as the great classic of Kabbalah, on a par with the Torah and Talmud as an authoritative expression of orthodox Jewish thought. And since Shimon bar Yochai was the hero of the "Zohar", he came to eclipse Akiva in the eyes of the Kabbalists as the supreme example of a rabbi who upheld Jewish tradition and defied the Romans in the time of the "Jewish Wars". It was clearly for this reason that he eventually replaced Akiva as the central character in the celebration of Lag BaOmer. The various pretexts which were given for associating him with this holiday were all more or less imaginary, but they were accepted because behind them stood the actual fact that he had evaded Roman persecution.

Liebes, on page 39 of *Studies in the Zohar*, argues that behind the figure of Shimon bar Yochai in the "Zohar" also stood the figure of Simon bar Kochba. He states:

Furthermore, it could be that the *Zohar*'s author associated

132

Bar-Kokhba's first name, Simeon, with that of his hero and consequently endowed Bar Yohai with some of Bar-Kokhba's characteristics. To be sure, R. Simeon and his companions in the *Zohar* were not warriors like Bar-Kokhba and his men, but their association with the latter may well have been among the reasons for the metaphorical description of the participants at the *Idra* bearing weapons and decked in armor.

The founders of the state of Israel came to a similar conclusion. Rahel Yanait Ben-Zvi, a member of Ben-Gurion's inner circle, describes in her memoirs, *Coming Home*, the fascination which they all felt with the memory of Bar Kochba. She states on page 128 that she wrote a pamphlet about Bar Kochba around 1908 and distributed it on Lag BaOmer, "the festival connected with Bar-Kochba". Due in large part to the influence of Ben-Gurion and his circle, Lag BaOmer has come to be regarded in Israel as a celebration of the accomplishments of Simon bar Kochba. The custom of lighting bonfires was appropriated from the Kabbalists and Hasidim but transferred to the open countryside in memory of the guerilla war which Bar Kochba and his followers had fought. The modern Israeli tradition of celebrating Lag BaOmer in the open countryside is also a continuation of a Jewish folk custom from Eastern Europe, where boys on Lag BaOmer would go into the woods and play with bows and arrows.

It is very possible that all of the diverse traditions relating to Lag BaOmer are ultimately derived from an actual historic event, the liberation of Jerusalem from the Romans by the forces of Simon bar Kochba. Coins issued by Bar Kochba's government commemorated the liberation of Jerusalem, and this may well have taken place on the 18th of Iyar, the date on which Lag BaOmer always falls on the Jewish calendar. After the defeat of Bar Kochba and his subsequent denigration as a "false Messiah" in the Talmud, it became politically impossible to celebrate the 18th of Iyar as a victory of Bar Kochba, yet the rabbis wished to preserve its memory all the same. Connecting Lag BaOmer first with

Akiva and then with Shimon bar Yochai was an effective way of doing this. Bar Kochba himself was concealed from view, yet inasmuch as both Akiva and Bar Yochai had been associated with him and supported him, celebrating Lag BaOmer in their name also kept alive in a hidden form the memory of what must have been regarded at the time as his greatest accomplishment, the restoration, however brief, of Jewish rule in Jerusalem. And in general, the tremendous prestige of both Akiva and Shimon bar Yochai in rabbinical tradition would seem to be due in large part to their association with Bar Kochba. Neither one was actually responsible for any great innovations in Jewish law or philosophy, but they became role models for later generations of rabbis because they had proven their dedication to Jewish freedom and independence by their support for the revolt led by Bar Kochba. It was too dangerous to say this openly, however, and therefore they were credited with a whole set of fictional accomplishments instead - Akiva with ascent to heaven in a chariot, Bar Yochai with the mystical theories of the "Zohar".

What this analysis suggests is that the main reason why the concept of "the Messiah" acquired a canonical status in rabbinical thought during the Talmudic period is because Akiva had hailed Simon bar Kochba as "King Messiah". This action on the part of the leading rabbi of the day was too definitive to go back on. The application of the title of Messiah to Bar Kochba had to be rescinded because he was defeated and killed, but there could be no going back on the underlying idea that the Jewish people would be liberated by "the Messiah". To repudiate that thought would be to repudiate Akiva as well, and this the rabbinical establishment was unwilling to do. Instead the authors of the "literature of the chariot" populated Akiva's heaven with gigantic supernatural beings who could easily be seen as imaginary representations of the type of person whom the rabbis imagined Bar Kochba to have been. In Kabbalistic tradition, the concept of the Golem came to serve a similar function. The Golem was an imaginary creature with immense physical strength whom various rabbis were credited with having brought to life by magical means. Under the control of a rabbi, his strength was to be used on

134

behalf of the Jewish people. Simon bar Kochba in the Talmud is pictured in similar terms as an amazingly powerful individual who was said to catch the huge stones which the Romans launched at him and hurl them back at them. But according to the Talmud, he fought with the rabbis and was therefore defeated. The Golem could be seen as an improved version of Simon bar Kochba, a giant who didn't talk back. The real Simon bar Kochba is hard to locate in the midst of all this imagery, but there can be little doubt that he was the original role model for the Unknown Messiah.

What took place in modern times was a kind of bifurcation between the overt content of the rabbinical image of the Messiah and its covert meaning. The secular Zionists who actually settled in the land of Israel in the 20th century and built up a Jewish army there looked to Simon bar Kochba as a role model. They did not declare themselves believers in "the Messiah", yet they nonetheless developed a cult of Simon bar Kochba, fabricating a number of legends around him to embellish his rather sketchy historical memory and turning Lag Ba'Omer into a national holiday. Meanwhile the rabbis who opposed secular Zionism as a blasphemous attempt to "force the end" placed more and more emphasis on the miraculous, otherworldly, supernatural quality of the Messianic ideal. The closer the actual "ingathering of the exiles" in the land of Israel came to resemble the Messianic promise, the more the Orthodox establishment came to insist on the performance of miracles as the indispensable proof of the advent of the Messiah. Paradoxically, those who actually did what the Messiah was supposed to do showed little or no interest in claiming Messianic status, while those who remained at home and poured scorn on the Zionist enterprise claimed thereby to affirm the intensity of their belief in the coming of the Messiah. This strange paradox was rooted in the dual character of the traditional rabbinical Messianic ideal, resolutely supernaturalist in its external form yet with an inner core that hearkened back to the actual deeds of the unknown Messiah, Simon bar Kochba.

But why did the secular Zionists, who were more than dimly aware of the true meaning of traditional Jewish Messianism, not claim Messianic status for themselves? Their problem is that the Messianic ideal had become so encrusted with supernatural elements that a secular form of Messianism could not proclaim itself as such. To claim Messianic status in any way, shape or form was inevitably to invite the charge of trickery due to the close association between Messianism and supernaturalism. The writings and public pronouncements of the Zionists who founded the state of Israel are filled with subtle allusions to the Messianic character of their movement, but this connection was rarely stated too explicitly, nor did any secular Zionist leader ever consider claiming Messianic status for themselves. Nonetheless, it is abundantly clear that the secular Zionists, and David Ben-Gurion in particular, were intensely conscious of the fact that they were doing what the Messiah was supposed to do. Moreover, it is also clear that they were motivated to do this at least in part by the influence of the Jewish Messianic tradition on their own belief system. That tradition proclaimed in no uncertain terms that the task of the Messiah was to bring about the ingathering of the exiles and the establishment of a Jewish state in the land of Israel, and that is precisely what the secular Zionists set out to do and did in fact accomplish. Various factors led them to do this, of which the Messianic tradition was only one, yet it is highly doubtful that they would have embarked upon the Zionist enterprise were it not for this tradition.

Furthermore, the secular Zionists did not merely aim at the ingathering of the exiles and the establishment of a Jewish state, but they also sought to embody another aspect of the Messianic tradition, the belief in the advent of a more equitable, just and compassionate society not only in the land of Israel but throughout the entire world. They were, after all, in their majority members of the international socialist movement and regarded themselves as social revolutionaries. As has often been observed, their socialist convictions were but a secularized version of the traditional belief that the coming of the Messiah would inaugurate an era of unprecedented peace and harmony on a worldwide scale. This belief can be documented in rabbinic literature, but its main bulwark was in Jewish popular culture. Messianic beliefs were transmitted through this culture in an even more elusive form than in rabbinic culture, since popular culture relied far more on oral tradition than on written texts. Songs and legends about the Messiah abounded, some of which were later collected in anthologies like *Voices Of A People* by Ruth Rubin. On page 139 appears the following verse from a song about Elijah, the forerunner of the coming of the Messiah in popular tradition:

> Elijah the prophet comes into our house,
> And tells us good news, and brings good tidings:
> All the lame shall walk straight again,
> All the poor shall become rich,
> All the sick shall be healed,
> All the naked shall be clothed,
> All the heavy, bitter hearts
> Shall be uplifted, dear God.

The socialist Zionists were motivated by these beliefs at least as much if not more than the religious, since they tried to create an institutional framework in which all these things would actually come to pass. From their point of view, the importance of the Messianic ideal lay less in the expectation of a miraculous Savior than it did in the utopian and revolutionary ideals which traditionally surrounded this expectation.

Nonetheless the expectation of the advent of some kind of victorious leader, be he human, divine or some mixture of the two, was so integral to the Messianic ideal that no version of this ideal could entirely dispense with it. The socialist Zionists made every effort to stress the collective character of their movement and their disdain for what was later to be called "the cult of the personality", yet David Ben-Gurion gradually became their recognized leader and came to enjoy a status in Israeli culture that was not without a certain Messianic tinge. From King David to David Ben-Gurion, the Jewish Messianic ideal was first and foremost a belief in a successful leader. It was for this reason that Simon bar Kochba could not be remembered as "the Messiah" in Jewish tradition, for he did not ultimately prove successful. All the same, it seems clear that it was his influence more than any other which resulted in the elevation of the concept of "the Messiah" to canonical status in later rabbinical culture. The question therefore inevitably arises: just who was Simon bar Kochba? What was he like as a person? What were his beliefs, and what was the character of the movement he led? To what extent was the Messianic ideal in later

137

Jewish tradition shaped by his influence? These questions are almost impossible to answer due to the paucity of the source material, and yet without a picture of Simon bar Kochba no analysis of the origins of the Messianic ideal could be complete. Unknown he remains, yet known he must be.

Bar Kosiba

Simon bar Kochba, it turns out, was actually named Simon (or Shimon, or Shimeon) bar Kosiba. The name "Kochba" was an allusion to his Messianic status. It was remembered mainly due to the presence of references to "bar Kochba" as the leader of the second revolt against Rome in the works of several early Christian writers. "Kochba" means "star" in Hebrew and is associated with the verse, "And a star shall come forth out of Jacob", which was traditionally viewed as a Messianic prophecy. In the Talmud on the other hand he is generally called "bar (or "ben") Koziba". Koziba means "deceiver" and the authors of the Talmud obviously called him this in order to emphasize their claim that he was a "false Messiah". "Bar" or "ben" mean "son", or in this context, "son of". Jewish men were generally known by their first name, followed by the expression, "son of", followed by their father's name. Only in modern times has it become clear that the names "bar Kochba" and "bar Koziba" were both applied to him as a form of word play based on his original name, "bar Kosiba".

This information became known as a result of the discovery in the 1950s and 1960s of a number of letters sent by Simon bar Kochba to followers of his in Ein Gedi, a fertile oasis situated near the shores of the Dead Sea. In flight from the Romans, these followers of bar Kochba subsequently took refuge in remote caves in the walls of ravines not far from Ein Gedi. The Romans trapped them in the caves, where they presumably starved to death. Their personal belongings, along with the letters and also their bones, were preserved in the caves for nearly 2000 years due to the dry climate of the Dead

Sea area and the inaccessibility of the caves. Most of the letters were discovered in 1960 by an Israeli archaeological expedition commanded by Yigael Yadin, who had previously been one of the main leaders of the Jewish forces during the War of Independence in 1948. Yadin subsequently published a book, *Bar-Kokhba*, which is undoubtedly the most important source of information about both the letters and bar Kochba now available.

In the letters, reports Yadin, bar Kochba is generally called "Shimeon bar Kosiba, President of Israel". The term, "President of Israel", also appears on many of the coins issued by bar Kochba's government, which have been unearthed in large numbers throughout the land of Israel. On the coins, however, the name "bar Kosiba" never appears, but only "Shimeon". The Hebrew word which Yadin translates as "President" is "nasi". In modern Hebrew, the president of Israel is called "nasi", as are the presidents of other countries, including the United States. But when used in ancient Hebrew texts, the word "nasi" is usually translated as "prince". It has no religious connotations and is definitely not associated in any way with the concept of Messiah. Whether "president" or "prince", it connotes a secular head of state. This is a significant point, because it shows that even though he may have been regarded as "King Messiah" by rabbi Akiba, Simon bar Kochba actually presented himself, both on his coins and in his letters, as a secular ruler.

Another usage found both on the coins and the letters is typified by such expressions as "Year One of the Redemption of Israel", "Year Two of the Freedom of Israel" or "the third year of Shimeon bar Kosiba, President of Israel". There was no fourth year. The revolt led by bar Kochba is thought to have taken place between 132 and 135 CE, which fits in with the evidence of the coins and letters. The practice of counting years from the start of the reign of a king or emperor was an ancient one, and it was employed by the Roman Caesars among others. The fact that it was used by bar Kochba and his followers suggests that they viewed him in a similar light. However he was never called "king" in the coins or letters and there is no reason to think that he claimed this title. It would seem that he sought to exercise an authority similar to that of a king but deliberately avoided the use of this term for one reason or another. The main emphasis, as reflected in expressions like "Year One of the Redemption of Israel", was on the start of his reign as the inauguration of a new era in Jewish history.

A further indication of the type of authority claimed by bar Kochba is provided by the numerous passages in the letters which deal with land transactions in Ein Gedi. As Yadin notes on page 239, Ein Gedi had previously been considered "crown property" under the Romans "because of its wealth in spices, particularly the famous balsam". It is apparent from the letters that bar Kochba also claimed the land of Ein Gedi as the property of his administration, or as Yadin puts it, "nationalized" it. Individual plots of land were then leased to various individuals for a fee, and these individuals then further sub-leased portions of their property, also for a fee. A large part of the letters is devoted to these various transactions, and it may well be for this reason that they were retained by the followers of bar Kochba, who undoubtedly hoped to return to their property in Ein Gedi when and if the Romans were defeated. It is mainly with these transactions in mind that Yadin refers on page 182 to "the elaborate system of Bar-Kokhba's administration". This system was evidently modeled to some extent on the Roman system which had preceded it, but with patriotic Jews rather than Hellenizing collaborators as its main beneficiaries.

That bar Kochba's followers were also religious Jews is shown by a number of indications. One letter found in the caves contains a request by bar Kochba to his followers in Ein Gedi to deliver to him a sizable quantity of the "four kinds" of vegetation used for the holiday of Succot. Two donkeys were provided by bar Kochba for this purpose. He explained in the letter that he needed the "four kinds" so that the men in his army could celebrate Succot properly. Also, among the artifacts found in the caves were metal utensils of Roman manufacture which the followers of bar Kochba had used for cooking and food storage. All of the images of pagan figures which appeared on the utensils had been filed down and defaced by bar Kochba's followers. Textile fragments were also found in the caves, and as Yadin puts it on page 66: "The clothing and other woven material showed

that the weavers and wearers of these were very orthodox Jews."
This is because, in accordance with Jewish law, diverse fibers were
never mixed together in the same piece of cloth.

On the other hand, there is very little direct expression of
religious sentiment in any of the letters. The name of God is
never invoked, and the implied emphasis is more on patrio-
tism than religion. One letter, cited by Yadin on page 133,
concludes with the following reproach from bar Kochba to his
followers in Ein Gedi: "In comfort you sit, eat and drink from
the property of the House of Israel, and care nothing for your
brothers." Yadin comments:

> Lastly, an interesting point emerging from this letter is that
> the Bar-Kokhba fighters used to refer to each other as 'broth-
> ers', a usage not uncommon in revolutionary movements.

There is also a passage from the Talmud, cited by Yadin on
page 26, that states, with reference to the followers of bar
Kochba: "When they went forth to battle, they cried: [Oh God!]
Neither help us nor disgrace us." In the eyes of the authors of
the Talmud, this was evidence of their impious and blasphemous attitude. Putting two and two together, it would seem
that although bar Kochba and his followers were definitely
religious Jews, religion was not the main force which bound
them together.

To some extent that force was military. The one point on
which all versions of bar Kochba agree is that he was a for-
midable military commander. Hadrian's troops, on returning
to Rome from the Second Jewish War, omitted the custom-
ary declaration that they were well, so heavy were the casualties which they suffered in combat with the forces of bar
Kochba. Eusebius, a Christian writer, reported that bar
Kochba executed Christians who refused to fight in his army.
The Talmud, notes Yadin on page 23, contains "a story of his
practice to test the prowess of his soldiers by cutting off their
fingers". The letters found by Yadin paint a similar picture.
As Yadin puts it on page 124:

141

> If style is any criterion by which to judge men's character, then Bar-Kokhba seems to have been a strong and tough man, not unlike his description in the Jewish sources. The letters are written in an abrupt - even telegraphic - style. Most demands and orders are coupled with an admonition.

By "admonition", Yadin actually means "threat". If his orders are not carried out, warns bar Kochba in one letter, "I will put fetters on your feet as I did to ben Aphlul." It would seem that the ultimate basis of bar Kochba's authority among Jews was the perception that this man was strong enough and tough enough to conceivably defeat the Romans.

What was he like as a person? The only clue that emerges from the letters is that they were all written in different hands and also in three different languages - Hebrew, Aramaic and Greek. It seems evident that the letters were not actually written by bar Kochba himself but by scribes to whom he dictated their contents. Was he perhaps illiterate? No one knows for sure. Literally nothing is known of bar Kochba's origins, of his personal history or of the process through which he became "prince" or "president" of Israel. Even after the discovery of the letters, Yadin's description, on page 27, of bar Kochba's traditional image in Jewish culture still remains essentially true:

> But when all the fragmentary tales and traces of Bar-Kokhba were assembled they amounted to no more than the lineaments of a ghost. He figured in Jewish folklore more as a myth than a man of flesh and blood, as impersonal as a Hercules or a King Arthur. It was centuries of persecution of the Jews and their yearning for national rehabilitation that turned Bar-Kokhba into a people's hero - an elusive figure they clung to because he had demonstrated, and was the last to demonstrate, that the Jews could fight to win spiritual and political independence.

Even the manner of his death remains unknown. It is assumed that he was killed when the Romans stormed Betar, the last stronghold of his forces, but no one knows for sure. One of the letters found by Yadin was in poor condition and only a few phrases were legible. He cites these, on page 139, as follows: "till the end",

142

"they have no hope", "my brothers in the south", "of these were lost by the sword" and "these my brothers". Like the partisans in the Warsaw ghetto, bar Kochba fought a hopeless fight to the bitter end, and from this struggle a myth was born.

There is no way to know the man behind the myth except to imagine him. Who precisely was Simon bar Kosiba? It is highly unlikely that he came from a priestly or wealthy family. The fact that he made no claim to religious authority suggests that he did not have much of a religious education, which in turn suggests that he came from a lower class background. His military ability suggests a rural rather than urban background, for farmers were more accustomed to strenuous physical activity than artisans. Betar, his last stronghold, is located a little to the south and west of Jerusalem, which he also held for some time based on the evidence of his coins. It would seem therefore that he came from the southern part of the country and specifically the territory of the former kingdom of Judah in which both Betar and Jerusalem were located. He seems to have used guerilla tactics against the Romans, suggesting a familiarity with the countryside in the south. It is tempting to imagine him as a shepherd just like David before him, for the herding of sheep and goats was more characteristic of the rural economy of the south than it was of the north. In any case, if he had a role model, it was very likely king David. David too, unlike the Maccabees and Zealots, had made no claim to religious authority and was essentially a military leader. Growing up in the same territory as David had come from, possibly pursuing the same occupation, Simon bar Kosiba could easily have thought himself destined to do what David had done - drive out the foreign invaders and unify the country under his leadership.

The little that is reliably known about Simon bar Kosiba suggests that he did in fact have a conscious concern with unity. It is evident from the works of Josephus that one of the main reasons for the defeat of the Jewish forces in the first Jewish War was their extreme disunity and infighting among themselves. Simon bar Kosiba must have noticed this too, and it is remarkable to what extent he was able to create a united front against the Romans. Some of his coins bear the inscription, "Eleazar the priest", suggesting that despite the destruction of the

Temple bar Kosiba had enlisted the surviving priestly class in support of his movement. Akiva's salutation of him as "King Messiah" shows that he was supported by the Pharisees as well. Both the coins and the letters suggest that he possessed a degree of personal authority which no leader of the first revolt had succeeded in attaining. This authority was most likely based not only on his military ability but also his political skill. By not claiming religious authority and by avoiding the title of "king", he was able to avoid many of the controversies and schisms which had befallen the Maccabees and Zealots before him. His religious ideas seem to have been entirely conventional without any hint of sectarian ideology. In short, his message was clear and simple: unite behind his leadership, drive out the Romans and reestablish the nation of Judah in the traditional mold, with a Temple, a High Priest and a secular ruler, perhaps a "prince" today and a "king" tomorrow.

Given the history of the Messianic ideal, it seems very clear that Simon bar Kosiba had little or no desire to become "the Messiah". Yet what survived of his struggle was, on the one hand, the memory that he had fought the Romans to the bitter end, and on the other hand, the memory that Akiva had hailed him as "King Messiah". From this combination of circumstances arose the secret history of Simon bar Kochba as the unknown Messiah, the hidden reason why Akiva and Shimon bar Yochai became rabbinical cult figures and why the concept of the advent of "the Messiah" became henceforth an article of faith in Jewish rabbinical culture. What bar Kochba had accomplished could neither be affirmed nor denied. He had done what "the Messiah" was supposed to do, yet in the end he had been defeated and killed. Jewish rabbinical culture dealt with this paradox by treating him personally as a "false Messiah" while at the same time closing ranks behind the concept of the advent of "the Messiah" as the preordained culmination of Jewish history. From this time forward, no other word for an awaited redeemer is to be found in Jewish literature. Perhaps the Christian emphasis on Jesus as "the Messiah" also played a role here, but this emphasis may itself have been conditioned by the disappearance of other terms for an awaited redeemer in Jewish literature after 135 CE. In the New Testament, the term "son of man" is often used to designate Jesus as a Messianic figure, and it was apparently only gradually that "the Messiah" became the official term. Most likely there was a complex interaction between Jewish and Christian versions of the Messianic ideal which led both sides to gradually unite behind the term "the Messiah" as the only possible designation for an awaited redeemer.

In the Jewish version, what was extrapolated from bar Kochba the actual person was the abstract ideal of strength. Strength is the theme which permeates the legend of bar Kochba in Jewish tradition, and strength is also the dominant characteristic of the mythical Messianic figures, such as Metatron or the Golem, who are to be found in later rabbinical literature. But in the official rabbinical conception of "the Messiah" as a heavenly figure awaiting God's permission to redeem the Jewish people, strength was not a major component. The supernatural Messiah of rabbinical tradition did not need strength for God himself could be counted on to do all the heavy lifting associated with the "end of days". To the contrary, the main characteristic of the rabbinical Messiah was compassion. He is frequently pictured as feeling the suffering of the Jewish people and anxious to act on their account for this reason. Here too Christian influence cannot be discounted, although there is little or no trace of the Christian concept of a physically suffering Messiah in the rabbinical version. The suffering of the rabbinical Messiah is entirely vicarious. He knows what the Jewish people endures and is only waiting them for them to repent and fulfill the commandments in the right way so that God can allow him to carry out his task of bringing about the ingathering of the exiles and the restoration of the nation of Judah. Only in a concealed and subterranean form did an alternate conception persist that, as Jabotinsky once put it, "strength is the only consolation".

Forcing the End

In rabbinical literature, the use of strength to try to bring about the ingathering of the exiles in advance of God's command came to be known as "forcing the end". Avraham Stern, the founder of LEHI (Fighters for the Freedom of Israel), actually used this term in his writings and poetry. LEHI was the first Jewish organization in the land of Israel to take up arms against the British, beginning its struggle for Jewish independence in 1940 despite the fact that the British were then at war with the Nazis. Stern and many of his followers were avowed Messianists who believed that only by "forcing the end" could the Messiah be made to appear. Joseph Heller, on page 83 of *The Stern Gang*, characterizes the views of Stern and his "circle" in 1940 as follows:

> A 'terrible' world war would ensue on the appearance of the herald of the Messiah, after which the Messiah himself would appear and establish the rule of the Hebrew nation over the entire world. 'Realists' believed that the Messiah must be helped by channeling the desire of the nation into the correct grooves and by awakening the people to correct action in order to throw off the foreign yoke. Authorization for this teaching was found in the writings of Maimonides, who had stated that the messianic king was not expected to work miracles such as the resurrection of the dead. Rather, he was to be judged according to his success in defeating the neighboring peoples, rebuilding the Temple and gathering in the Jews who were scattered throughout the world.

Heller was not sympathetic to LEHI, and it may be that he exaggerates the religious component in their thought in this passage, but there is no doubt that Stern's ideology was permeated with Messianic elements. Stern himself was murdered by the British in 1942, but LEHI continued its armed struggle, eventually inspiring other and larger Jewish organizations to join in. There was thus a direct connection between a fairly overt form of Messianism and the movement which eventually resulted in the ouster of the British and the proclamation of the state of Israel in 1948.

The thing is, forcing the end was always inherent in the rabbinical conception of the Messiah despite the numerous attempts in rabbinical literature to disavow any such intent. The rabbinical conception of bringing the Messiah by correct performance of the mitzvot kept hope alive but could not possibly succeed. The more sincere the believer in the rabbinical doctrine, the more apparent its ultimate ineffectiveness. Thus the ambition to force the end arose from the heart of rabbinical culture and was already apparent in the theory and practice of Kabbalah long before the rise of secular Zionism. The Kabbalists sought to force the end by magico-mystical techniques and also by settling in the land of Israel once the rise of the Ottoman empire made it possible to do so. Secular Zionism was merely a continuation of this tendency, one which dispensed entirely with the belief in miracles and translated the belief in the coming of the Messiah into a practical program for the settlement, cultivation and conquest of the land of Israel. As David Ben-Gurion stated over and over in his published writings, secular Zionism was nothing other than Jewish Messianism in a modern garb. Ben-Gurion criticized the passivity and ineffectiveness of the rabbinical Messianic tradition but never doubted that his own ideas were a direct outgrowth of this same tradition. Like most of the founders of the state of Israel, he was steeped in traditional Jewish culture and specifically the Hebrew language religious culture from which the Hebrew language secular culture of the state of Israel is derived. He viewed Messianism as the key idea of this religious culture, and indeed it was.

To put it another way, Messianism was nothing other than the idea of the restoration of the nation of Judah stated in a more or less metaphoric and visionary form. Stripped of its metaphoric and visionary elements, Messianism became Zionism. But implicit in Zionism, as in Messianism, was also Isaiah's insight that the cause of the nation of Judah was inseparable from the cause of the ideals which it sought to embody. Both Messianism and Zionism implied therefore not only the restoration of the nation of Judah but also the triumph of the ideals of justice, compassion and rationality on a world scale. This is what actually happened with the defeat of the Nazis in World War Two, and it was no coincidence that the birth of the nation of Israel came about as a direct result of the triumph of the wartime Allies over the Nazis. The ideals of the Allies, whether communist, socialist, democratic or liberal, were also the ideals of the Zionist movement, and they were put into practice by the state of Israel in the form of a democratic socialist political and economic system. This too was but a secular translation of the Messianic ideal with its traditional emphasis, particularly in Jewish

147

popular culture, upon the social transformation which would take place as a result of the advent of the Messiah.

The Messianic ideal fostered the birth of Israel not only directly, through its influence on the modern Zionist movement, but also indirectly, through its influence on the communist, socialist, democratic and liberal movements of modern times. Common to all these movements is the belief that human progress is possible, that the age old problems of poverty, war and injustice can eventually be solved and that the human race can ultimately achieve peace and prosperity on a global scale. This belief is but a secular reformulation of the Messianic ideal that was perpetuated in Christian tradition under the rubric of the "Second Coming". And the concept of the "Second Coming" is really just a restatement of standard Jewish Messianism in a form compatible with Christian doctrine. Throughout the pre-modern period, this concept played a key role in stimulating Messianic movements throughout the European continent which in turn created the basis for the secular progressive movements of the past 200 years. The Nazi assault in World War Two was an attempt to destroy these movements once and for all, and it was for this reason that the Nazis launched their genocidal attack on the Jewish people in this same context. It was the Jewish people who created the Messianic ideal and sustained it over centuries, and it is the Jewish people who will continue to uphold the banner of human progress through the coming centuries come what may.

Select Bibliography

Donald Harmon Akenson, Surpassing Wonder: The Invention of the Bible and the Talmuds (New York: 1998)

William Albright, Yahweh and the Gods of Canaan (Garden City: 1968)

Gedaliah Alon, The Jews In Their Land In The Talmudic Age (Cambridge: 1989)

Samuel Angus, The Mystery Religions and Christianity (New York: 1925)

Michael Avi-Yonah, The Jews of Palestine (New York: 1978)

Michael Baigent & Richard Leigh, The Dead Sea Scrolls Deception (London:1996)

Ernst Bammel & C.F.D. Moule, eds., Jesus and the Politics of His Day (Cambridge: 1984)

David Ben-Gurion, Ben-Gurion Looks At The Bible (New York: 1972)

David Ben-Gurion, Ben-Gurion Looks Back In Talks With Moshe Pearlman (New York: 1965)

Haim-Hillel Ben-Sasson, ed., A History of the Jewish People (Cambridge: 1976)

Rachel Yanait Ben-Zvi, Coming Home (Tel Aviv: 1963)

Jeremy Bentham, Not Paul, But Jesus (London: 1823)

Elias Bickerman, From Ezra to the Last of the Maccabees (New York: 1962)

Monette Bohrman, Flavius Josephus, the Zealots and Yavneh (Bern: 1994)

S.G.F. Brandon, The Fall of Jerusalem and the Christian Church (London: 1951)

S.G.F. Brandon, Jesus and the Zealots (New York: 1967)

John Bright, Early Israel In Recent History Writing (Chicago: 1956)

Edward Campbell, "The Amarna Letters and the Amarna Period", in The Biblical Archaeologist, Vol. XXIII (1960)

George Carter, Zoroastrianism and Judaism (Boston: 1918)

R.H. Charles, The Apocrypha and Pseudepigrapha of the Old Testament in English, 2 Vols. (Oxford: 1913)

James Charlesworth, ed., The Messiah: Developments in Earliest Judaism and Christianity (Minneapolis: 1992)

James Charlesworth, ed., The Old Testament Pseudepigrapha, 2 Vols. (New York: 1983-85)

James Charlesworth, The Pseudepigrapha and Modern Research (Chico: 1981)

Norman Cohn, The Pursuit of the Millenium (New York: 1970)

John Collins, Between Athens and Jerusalem (New York: 1983)

Franz Cumont, The Oriental Religions in Roman Paganism (New York: 1956)

Franz Cumont, Astrology and Religion Among the Greeks and Romans (New York: 1960)

Joseph Dan, The Ancient Jewish Mysticism (Tel Aviv: 1993)

Alan Davies, ed., Antisemitism and the Foundations of Christianity (New York: 1979)

Glanville Downey, Ancient Antioch (Princeton: 1963)

Samuel Eddy, The King Is Dead: Studies In Near Eastern Resistance to Hellenism (Lincoln: 1961)

Robert Eisenman, Maccabees, Zadokites, Christians and Qumran (Leiden: 1983)

Isidore Epstein, Judaism: A Historical Presentation (England: 1959)

William Reuben Farmer, Maccabees, Zealots, and Josephus (Westport: 1973)

Louis Feldman & Gohei Hata, eds., Josephus, Judaism, and Christianity (Detroit: 1987)

Louis Finkelstein, Akiba (New York: 1978)

Louis Finkelstein, The Pharisees (Philadelphia: 1938)

David Flusser, Judaism and the Origins of Christianity (Jerusalem: 1988)

Henri Frankfort, Kingship and the Gods (Chicago: 1948)

Henri Frankfort, Ancient Egyptian Religion (New York: 1948)

P.M. Fraser, Ptolemaic Alexandria (Oxford: 1972)

James Frazer, The Golden Bough, Parts I-VI (London: 1966)

Erich Fromm, You Shall Be As Gods: A Radical Interpretation of the Old Testament (New York: 1966)

John Gager, The Origins of Anti-Semitism (New York: 1983)

Yehoshua Gitay, Isaiah and His Audience (Maastricht: 1991)

150

Yehoshua Gitay, Prophecy and Prophets (Atlanta: 1997)

Joscelyn Godwin, Mystery Religions in the Ancient World (London: 1981)

Norman Golb, Who Wrote The Dead Sea Scrolls? (New York: 1995)

Edgar Goodspeed, The Apocrypha: An American Translation (New York: 1959)

Edgar Goodspeed, The Story of the Bible (Chicago: 1936)

Norman K. Gottwald, The Hebrew Bible In Its Social World And In Ours (Atlanta: 1993)

Norman K. Gottwald, ed., The Bible And Liberation (Maryland: 1983)

R.M. Grant, Gnosticism and Early Christianity (New York: 1966)

Moshe Greenberg, "The Hab/piru", in American Oriental Series, Vol. 39 (1955)

Julius H. Greenstone, The Messiah Idea In Jewish History (Philadelphia: 1948)

J. Gwyn Griffiths, The Origins of Osiris (Berlin: 1966)

W.K.C. Guthrie, The Greeks and Their Gods (Boston: 1950)

W.K.C. Guthrie, Orpheus and Greek Religion (New York: 1966)

Baruch Halpern, The Emergence of Israel in Canaan (Chico: 1983)

Gaston Halsberghe, The Cult of Sol Invictus (Leiden: 1972)

E.W. Heaton, Solomon's New Men (New York: 1974)

Joseph Heller, The Stern Gang (London: 1995)

Martin Hengel, The Zealots (Edinburgh: 1989)

Abraham Heschel, Maimonides (New York: 1982)

S.H. Hooke, ed., Myth, Ritual and Kingship (Oxford: 1958)

J. Phillip Hyatt, ed., The Bible In Modern Scholarship (Nashville: 1965)

Moshe Idel, Messianic Mystics (New Haven: 1998)

Jules Isaac, The Teaching of Contempt: Christian Roots of Anti-Semitism (New York: 1964)

King James Version, The New Testament (New York: n.d.)

Joachim Jeremias, The Eucharistic Words of Jesus (New York: 1966)

Jewish Publication Society, The Holy Scriptures According To The Masoretic Text (Philadelphia: 1955)

Jewish Publication Society, The Torah: The Five Books of Moses (Philadelphia: 1962)

D. Jobling, P. Day & G. Sheppard, eds., The Bible and the Politics of

Exegesis (Cleveland: 1991)

Hans Jonas, The Gnostic Religion (Boston: 1958)

Josephus, The Jewish War (England: 1939)

Josephus, The New Complete Works of Josephus
  (Grand Rapids: 1999)

Yehezkel Kaufmann, The Religion of Israel (Chicago: 1960)

David Katz & Richard Popkin, Messianic Revolution
  (New York: 1998)

G.D. Kilpatrick, The Eucharist In Bible And Liturgy
  (Cambridge: 1983)

Joseph Klausner, From Jesus To Paul (New York: 1943)

Joseph Klausner, Jesus of Nazareth (Boston: 1964)

Joseph Klausner, The Messiah Idea In Israel (New York: 1955)

Israel Knohl, The Messiah Before Jesus (Berkeley: 2000)

Emil Kraeling, Aram and Israel (New York: 1918)

F. Legge, Forerunners and Rivals of Christianity (New York: 1950)

Yehuda Liebes, Studies in Jewish Myth and Jewish Messianism
  (Albany: 1993)

Hyam Maccoby, Revolution In Judaea (New York: 1980)

Hyam Maccoby, The Sacred Executioner (New York: 1982)

Vittorio Macchioro, From Orpheus To Paul: A History of Orphism
  (New York: 1930)

Ramsay MacMullen, Constantine (New York: 1969)

Ramsay MacMullen, Enemies of the Roman Order
  (Cambridge: 1966)

Abraham Malherbe, Social Aspects of Early Christianity
  (Baton Rouge: 1977)

Wayne Meeks, The First Urban Christians (New Haven: 1963)

Doron Mendels, The Land of Israel As A Political Concept in
  Hasmonean Literature (Tubingen: 1987)

Doron Mendels, The Rise and Fall of Jewish Nationalism
  (New York: 1992)

George Mendenhall, "The Hebrew Conquest of Palestine", in The
  Biblical Archaeologist, Vol. XXV (1962)

George Mendenhall, The Tenth Generation: The Origins of the
  Biblical Tradition (Baltimore: 1973)

Samuel Mercer, The Tell El-Amarna Tablets (Toronto: 1939)

Arnold Meyer, Jesus or Paul? (London: 1909)

Arnaldo Momigliano, ed., The Conflict Between Paganism and
  Christianity in the Fourth Century (Oxford: 1963)

Sigmund Mowinckel, He That Cometh (New York: n.d.)

Gilbert Murray, Five Stages of Greek Religion (Westport: 1976)

B. Netanyahu, Don Isaac Abravanel (Ithaca: 1998)

Jacob Neusner, Death and Birth of Judaism (New York: 1987)

Jacob Neusner, The Four Stages of Rabbinic Judaism
  (London: 1999)

Jacob Neusner, Judaism: The Evidence of the Mishnah
  (Chicago: 1981)

Jacob Neusner, Judaism In Society (Chicago: 1983)

Jacob Neusner, Messiah In Context (Philadelphia: 1984)

Martin Nilsson, The Dionysiac Mysteries of the Hellenistic and
  Roman Age (Lund: 1957)

Martin Nilsson, "Early Orphism and Kindred Religious Movements",
  in Harvard Theological Review (July: 1935)

Martin Nilsson, A History of Greek Religion (Oxford: 1949)

Martin Noth, The History of Israel (New York: 1958)

Julian Obermann, "Calendaric Elements in the Dead Sea Scrolls", in
  Journal of Biblical Literature, Vol. LXXV (December: 1956)

Walter Otto, Dionysus, Myth and Cult (Bloomington: 1965)

Elaine Pagels, The Gnostic Gospels (New York: 1979)

James Parkes, The Conflict of the Church and the Synagogue
  (New York: 1974)

James Parkes, Jesus, Paul and the Jews (London: 1936)

Raphael Patai, The Messiah Texts (New York: 1979)

L. Patterson, Mithraism and Christianity (Cambridge: 1921)

Moshe Pearlman, The Zealots of Masada (New York: 1967)

Moshe Pearlman, The Maccabees (New York: 1973)

Stewart Perowne, Hadrian (New York: 1960)

Rafaele Pettazzoni, Essays on the History of Religions (Leiden: 1954)

Max Polley, Amos and the Davidic Empire (New York: 1989)

James Pritchard, The Ancient Near East, Vol. 1 (New York: 1958)

Hugo Rahner, Greek Myths and Christian Mystery (New York: 1971)

John Randall, Hellenistic Ways of Deliverance and the Making of the
  Christian Synthesis (New York: 1970)

Ellis Rivkin, A Hidden Revolution (Nashville: 1978)
Ellis Rivkin, The Shaping of Jewish History (New York :1971)
Archibald Robertson, The Origins of Christianity (New York: 1954)
James Robinson, ed., The Nag Hammadi Library in English
  (San Francisco: 1977)
Michael Rostovtzeff, Mystic Italy (New York: 1927)
Michael Rostovtzeff, The Social and Economic History of the Roman
  Empire (Oxford: 1957)
Rosemary Ruether, Faith and Fratricide: The Theological Roots of
  Anti-Semitism (New York: 1974)
D.S. Russell, The Jews From Alexander To Herod (London: 1967)
Samuel Sandmel, Judaism and Christian Beginnings (New York: 1978)
Hans-Joachim Schoeps, Jewish Christianity (Philadelphia: 1969)
Gershom Scholem, The Messianic Idea in Judaism and Other Essays
  on Jewish Spirituality (New York: 1971)
Hugh Schonfield, The Jesus Party (New York: 1974)
Emil Schurer, A History of the Jewish People in the Time of Jesus
  (New York: 1961)
Stephen Sharot, Messianism, Mysticism and Magic
  (Chapel Hill: 1982)
Henry Sheldon, The Mystery Religions and the New Testament
  (New York: 1918)
Grant Showerman, The Great Mother of the Gods (Chicago: 1969)
Joseph Sievers, The Hasmoneans and Their Supporters
  (Atlanta: 1990)
Daniel Silver & Bernard Martin, A History of Judaism
  (New York: 1974)
Friedrich Solmsen, Isis Among the Greeks and Romans
  (Cambridge: 1979)
John Stambaugh, Sarapis Under The Early Ptolemies (Leiden: 1972)
Menahem Stern, ed., Greek and Latin Authors on Jews and Judaism,
  Vol. 1 (Jerusalem: 1974)
Shemaryahu Talmon, King, Cult and Calendar In Ancient Israel
  (Jerusalem: 1986)
Victor Tcherikover, Hellenistic Civilization and the Jews
  (New York: 1977)
Alan Unterman, The Wisdom of the Jewish Mystics (New York: 1976)

Roland de Vaux, Ancient Israel (New York: 1966)

Maarten Vermaseren, Cybele and Attis (London: 1977)

Geza Vermes, The Dead Sea Scrolls In English (England: 1962)

John Warden, ed., Orpheus: The Metamorphosis of a Myth (Toronto: 1982)

William Westermann, The Slave Systems of Greek and Roman Antiquity (Philadelphia: 1955)

Harold Willoughby, Pagan Regeneration: A Study of Mystery Initiations (Chicago: 1929)

John Wilson, The Culture of Ancient Egypt (Chicago: 1951)

R.E. Witt, Isis In The Graeco-Roman World (Ithaca: 1971)

Robert Wolfe, Christianity In Perspective (New York: 1987)

Robert Wolfe, Dark Star (New York: 1984)

Yigael Yadin, Bar-Kokhba (New York: 1971)

Yigael Yadin, The Message of the Scrolls (New York: 1957)

Yigael Yadin, The Temple Scroll (New York: 1985)

Yigael Yadin, "The Temple Scroll - The Longest Dead Sea Scroll", in Shanks, ed., Understanding The Dead Sea Scrolls (New York: 1992)

R.C. Zaehner, The Dawn and Twilight of Zoroastrianism (New York: 1961)

Solomon Zeitlin, The Rise and Fall of the Jewish State, 3 Vols. (Philadelphia: 1968-78)

Solomon Zeitlin, Some Stages of the Jewish Calendar (n.p.: 1929)

Zoroaster, The Hymns of Zoroaster (London: 1914)